Bertram C. A. Windle

A Handbook of Surface Antomy and Landmarks

Bertram C. A. Windle

A Handbook of Surface Antomy and Landmarks

ISBN/EAN: 9783337815356

Printed in Europe, USA, Canada, Australia, Japan

Cover: Foto ©Andreas Hilbeck / pixelio.de

More available books at **www.hansebooks.com**

A HANDBOOK

OF

SURFACE ANATOMY

AND

LANDMARKS

BY

BERTRAM C. A. WINDLE, M.A., M.D. (Dubl.)

PROFESSOR OF ANATOMY IN THE QUEEN'S COLLEGE, BIRMINGHAM.

LONDON

H. K. LEWIS, 136 GOWER STREET, W.C.

1888

TO

PROFESSOR ALEXANDER MACALISTER,

M.A., M.D., F.R.S.

TO WHOM

AS A TEACHER AND A FRIEND

I OWE MORE THAN I CAN EXPRESS

PREFACE.

This little book is not a surgical applied anatomy. Had its author ever entertained any idea of writing such a work, he would certainly have abandoned it, as the ground is already occupied by Mr. Treves' excellent manual on that subject, to which he is indebted for various hints. This book is intended for anatomical students in their first and second years as a guide to that important portion of the knowledge of the human body which can be gained without the use of the scalpel and forceps. Junior students will find it useful after having first dissected a part of the body, to study the relations of the various structures as given herein on a fresh part, or still better, on the living subject. It is scarcely possible to impress too strongly upon the student desirous of obtaining a thorough practical knowledge of his profession, the importance of taking advantage of the opportunities afforded to him in the wards of the hospital and elsewhere, of familiarising himself with the surface markings, surgical and medical landmarks, and relations to the exterior of the important structures, in the living body.

Whilst not pretending to be a surgical anatomy properly so-called, certain surgical facts have from time to time been mentioned, where the importance of the anatomical point in question might be overlooked, without reference to its practical bearing. But the writer has preferred to err on the side of omission in this matter, lest the student should be confused by the introduction of too many unfamiliar facts.

Full directions have been given for the examination of certain of the orifices and for the use of some of the commoner surgical instruments, the author believing that it is of great value to the student to acquire a readiness and dexterity in handling them on the dead body, and that such should be learnt concurrently with the anatomical study of the parts in question.

It is difficult to exhibit any great originality in a work such as this (indeed much of what might be called original would inevitably be another name for incorrect), since the facts which are contained herein have mostly appeared in different manuals. To these it would be impossible to refer here in detail, but to their authors, whether their names are mentioned in the text or not, the writer desires to express his full acknowledgements. He has to thank his friend Dr. Crooke, Pathologist to the General Hospital in this town, for help in some of the details gained from the bodies in the post-mortem room of that Institution. Several careful dissections have been made in relation especially to the positions of certain of the thoracic and abdominal viscera, in order to ensure accuracy in the facts stated, and for assistance in these he has to thank his former pupil Mr. E. Teichelmann and his present pupils Messrs. A. R. Green and S. W. Warneford. He has also to thank his friend, Dr. Reid, for two blocks (Figs. 3 and 4).

Queen's College, Birmingham.

June 30th, 1888.

TABLE OF CONTENTS

Chapter I.

THE FACE.

Chapter II.

THE SCALP.

Chapter III.

THE NECK.

Chapter IV.

THE THORAX.

CONTENTS.

LIST OF FIGURES.

A HANDBOOK

OF

SURFACE ANATOMY.

CHAPTER I.

THE FACE.

I. The Face.

Bony points.—The forehead presents on either side two elevations, the frontal eminences, varying considerably in the amount of their development in different individuals. Below and separated from these by a shallow groove is a supra-ciliary ridge on each side, covered by the skin bearing the eyebrows. These ridges which also vary greatly in size may, but need not necessarily, owe their prominence to large cavities in the substance of the bone—the frontal sinuses. This is a fact of surgical importance, since a fracture of this ridge apparently deep and serious may not open up the cranial cavity, but only that of the sinus.

Like other air cavities in connection with the cranial and facial bones, these sinuses are small or non-existent in the young child, developing gradually in the course of growth. Between the supra-ciliary ridges is a flat smooth surface named the glabella, from which certain cranial measurements are made.

Each ridge is bounded at either extremity by a strong prominent angle, the outer of which is by far the better marked; these angles are the external and internal angular processes. The former limits anteriorly the temporal fossa, the temporal muscle which it contains, and the temporal ridge with its attached fascia.

By pushing up the skin covering the eyebrows, the supra-orbital notch may generally be felt at about the junction of the middle and internal thirds of the supraciliary ridge. This notch is sometimes replaced by a foramen, which may be situated somewhat deeply in the cavity of the orbit; its discovery is then more difficult, but it may be found by deep pressure. Through this notch or foramen pass the supra-orbital nerve and artery. The former, a branch of the ophthalmic division of the fifth nerve, is one of the common seats of facial neuralgia, for which complaint it may be necessary that it should be stretched or divided. Two other spots, at which branches of the fifth nerve emerge from bony canals, are of similar importance. The infra-orbital branch of the superior maxillary division emerges from the infra-orbital canal beneath the prominent ridge which forms the lower margin of the orbit. The infra-orbital foramen whose aperture looks inwards, is covered by muscles and cannot generally be felt from the surface. The same remark applies to the mental foramen situated in the inferior maxilla. Through this foramen which also looks inwards the mental branch of the inferior maxillary division of the fifth nerve escapes. The position of these two last mentioned foramina may be ascertained by drawing a line from the supra-orbital notch downwards and outwards so as to pass between both pairs of bicuspid teeth (*vide* fig. 1.)

This line will cross the infra-orbital foramen about a quarter of an inch below the margin of the orbit. The position of the mental foramen varies according to the age of the individual examined. In the child at puberty it is placed rather nearer to the lower than to the upper border of the jaw. In the adult it lies nearly midway between the two borders and about a quarter of an inch below the fold of mucous membrane passing from the jaw to the cheek inside the mouth. In old edentulous persons, owing to the disappearance of the alveoli from atrophy, the foramen is placed close to the upper margin of the jaw.

In the middle line of the face below the glabella the points to be noticed are the nasal bones with the cartilages attached to them, the nasal spine of the superior maxilla which can be felt between the openings of the nostrils, and the ridge at the centre of the inferior maxilla which marks the symphisis menti.

Following outwards, on either side, the lower margin of the orbit, the zygoma is reached and may be traced in its entire extent. The space between it and the cranial bones cannot be estimated in the undissected state, partly on account of the muscles which lie therein, and partly because of the firm and tense attachment of the temporal fascia above and of that of the parotid below. By passing the finger along the lower border of the zygoma, its tubercle may be distinguished immediately

in front of the outer part of the glenoid fossa and the
head of the inferior maxilla, the movements of which
latter can be distinctly felt, and, in a moderately thin
person, seen.

When the lower jaw is protruded its head will of
course be brought nearer to the tubercle; when a dislocation occurs it is carried still farther forward and
passes over the tubercle into the zygomatic fossa. Behind the head of the lower jaw the posterior root of the
zygoma may be felt passing above the external auditory
meatus.   In the region below the orbit the canine eminence may be distinguished, though not so clearly as
from within the mouth.   On its inner side is the inci-
sive fossa, on its outer, but at a higher level, the canine.

The greater portion of the inferior maxilla may be
defined by manipulation, the symphisis, body, posterior
portion of the ramus, head, and neck being all clearly
distinguishable. The coronoid process almost to its
apex may be felt by pressing the finger under the
zygoma and protruding and depressing the jaw.

Skin, etc.—The skin over the forehead is fairly
smooth and moveable, characteristics which it main-
tains as it covers the nose until it reaches the cartilaginous portion of that organ. Here its attachment
becomes much firmer, a fact which explains the great
pains caused by the small boils which form not unfrequently in the sebaceous follicles here very abundant.
In the remainder of the face the attachments of the
skin are loose save over the chin where its connections
with the deeper parts are somewhat greater.   It is this

laxity of attachment which permits of the great mobility of the skin under the influence of the numerous muscles connected with it and engaged in the production of the various expressions of the countenance.

The depth of the hollow under the zygoma varies greatly in different individuals, presenting all varieties from the plump rounded contour of the young girl to the hollow cheek of the emaciated sufferer from some wasting disease. This difference is due to the presence or absence of a pad of fat, the "buccal pellet" which lies beneath the zygoma and in front of the masseter under both of which structures it sends prolongations. In the adult this portion of adipose tissue is one of the first to disappear in wasting diseases.

In the child the pads of fat in the cheeks are much larger than in the adult, a fact to which is partly owing the comparative squareness of the infantile face. According to Symington, besides the subcutaneous fat there exists a mass "in the form of one or more lobules surrounded by a clearly defined capsule, so that it can be very easily shelled out." These masses have been called "sucking-cushions" from the assistance which they are supposed to lend the infant in performing that function.

These cushions diminish in the process of development until they come to be represented by the pellets first alluded to. According to Ranke they are only slightly decreased in size in emaciated children in whom the subcutaneous fat is almost entirely absent.

The skin of the face may be furrowed by various

lines, to some of which, when strongly marked, diagnostic importance has been attached. These lines individually and collectively differ greatly in the extent of their development in different persons. The most important of these furrows or wrinkles are :—1. The transverse rugæ of the forehead caused by the action of the occipito-frontal muscle. 2. The oculo-frontal rugæ passing vertically between the eyebrows to the root of the nose and due to the corrugator supercilii. 3. The linea oculo-zygomatica or line of Jadelot extending from the internal angle of the eye downwards and outwards to cross the face below the malar bone. This furrow is sometimes of a noticeably darker colour than the skin around it. 4. The naso-labial fold which commences between the side of the nose and the cheek, and passing obliquely downwards and outwards terminates near the commissure of the lips. It is almost always well-marked in old people. Lastly, so far as skin markings are concerned, the filtrum, a groove leading from the septum of the nose to the most prominent point of the upper lip, may be mentioned.

Blood-vessels.—The facial artery appears upon the face by crossing the inferior maxilla just in front of the masseter, where its pulsations may be felt and its flow checked by compression against the bone. It may again be felt in its tortuous course near the commissure of the lips, where it gives off the coronary artery of either lip, which can be distinguished running beneath the mucous membrane. Two other branches may also be made out, the lateralis nasi, a short distance above and external to the ala of the nose, and the angular artery, whose pulsations may be felt at the side of the root of the nose. This vessel and the anterior branch of the superficial temporal are of service to the anæsthetist, since they often enable him to feel his patient's pulse without incommoding the operator.

The supra-orbital artery emerges from the notch or foramen with the nerve of the same name, and passes towards the vertex of the head. Nearer to the inner angle of the orbit, the frontal artery escapes; this vessel is included in the root of the flap in the Indian operation for the restoration of a partly destroyed nose, and affords it nutriment.

The transverse facial artery, a branch of the superficial temporal, cannot be felt save when exceptionally large, but its position may be found by remembering that it crosses the face immediately above Steno's duct, to which attention will shortly be drawn.

The pulsations of the trunk of the superficial temporal artery may be felt where that vessel crosses the zygoma immediately in front of the external auditory meatus. Its anterior branch lies rather more than a finger's breadth behind the external angular process. (*Vide* fig. 1). This vessel is very liable to degeneration in old persons, in whom its tortuous trunk may be seen standing prominently out. Its pulsations also are very visible in some individuals, notably in those affected with incompetence of the aortic valves. It is the vessel which was divided in the now seldom performed operation of arteriotomy. The posterior branch lies about two inches behind the anterior, under cover of the hair.

The veins of the face are not of much importance so far as their surface relations are concerned. The vein which runs with the angular artery, a vessel of great importance from its intra-cranial connections, through the ophthalmic vein, is not unfrequently to be seen,

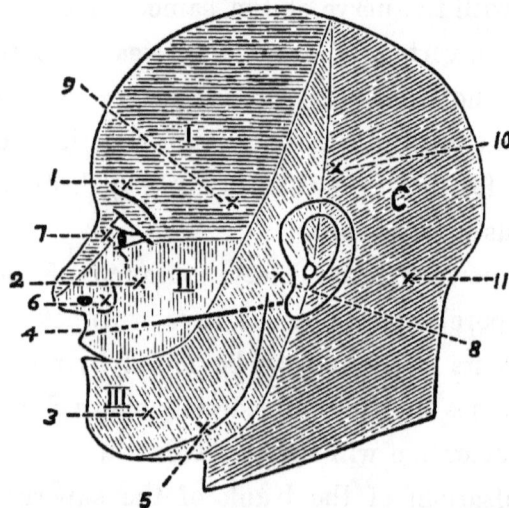

FIG. 1.—NERVOUS SUPPLY, ETC., OF FACE AND SCALP.

I. II. III. Regions supplied by the ophthalmic, superior and inferior maxillary divisions of the fifth nerve. C. Cervical nerves.

In this and succeeding similar figures it must, of course, be understood that the regions are not sharply marked off as would appear from the diagrammatic representation.

1, 2, 3, Points of exit of the supra- and infra-orbital and mental nerves. 4, Line of Steno's duct. 5, Point where facial artery crosses inferior maxilla. 6, Lateralis nasi. 7, Angular arteries. 8, Superficial temporal. 9, Anterior and 10, posterior branches. 11, Occipital artery.

and may be very distinct, especially in children. Some individuals possess an exceptionally large frontal vein on one side or the other, which may be seen standing

prominently out during laughter, etc. ; this vessel runs
vertically down near the centre of the forehead to join
the veins alluded to above.

Nerves.—The position of the three branches of the
fifth nerve has already been indicated in the description
of their foramina of exit.   The areas which they supply
will be seen by a reference to the diagram ; in connection with which it should be noted that the supply
of the upper part of the region belonging to the inferior
maxillary division is gained from the auriculo-temporal
nerve, which emerges from under cover of the parotid
gland and crosses the zygoma near the superficial
temporal artery.   The facial, the motor nerve of the
face, passes out of the substance of the parotid below
the duct of the latter, some of its branches, notably
that to the buccinator, running along the inferior
border of that structure.   The remainder ramify over
the face in lines more or less divergent from that of the
duct.

Other structures.—The parotid gland occupies a
space fairly well defined on each side, save its anterior
border, which lies for a variable extent upon the
masseter, and from which projects its only superficial
process, the socia parotidis, a portion which varies
considerably in size.   The body of the gland is limited
above by the zygoma.   Its inferior border may be
marked out by a line drawn from the angle of the jaw
to the mastoid process, whilst its posterior touches the
external auditory meatus, the mastoid process and the
sterno-mastoid muscle.   From the anterior border

emerges Steno's duct, which lies on the masseter below the socia parotidis. The position of the duct may be indicated by drawing a line from the point where the lobule joins the cartilage of the ear to a point midway between the nostrils and the red margin of the lips. About two inches of this line measured from the anterior border of the gland will correspond to the duct itself. (*Vide* fig. 1).

The student can readily ascertain its position in his own face by firmly clenching the jaws, when the masseter muscle will be tense and firmly contracted. By manipulating the central portion of the muscle with the points of the fingers the duct will easily be distinguished and will be recognised by its whip-cord like feel and by the flow of saliva into the mouth which generally follows its stimulation.

Before passing to the cavities associated with the face, it may be well to call the student's attention to the very common asymmetry of the two sides in one or more particulars. Hasse, from a very careful examination of the face of the celebrated Venus of Milo, found that whilst the portion lying below the nose was comparatively symmetrical, the upper part presented various deviations. Thus, the nose deviates to the left, the left ear stands higher than the right, the left half of the skull is broader than the right, and the left eye is higher and nearer the middle line than the right. He was led from this observation to examine carefully various skulls and heads of living individuals, and, as a result, states that whilst symmetry of the lower half of the face is the rule, deviations such as those occurring in the statue, commonly occur in the upper half.

II. The Eye and its Appendages.

Orbit.—The bony margin of the orbit has been already alluded to, and it need therefore only here be mentioned that for protective purposes the outer and upper portions are stronger and more prominent than the inner and lower, and especially the former. By tolerably deep pressure in the internal and superior angle the little projection to which the pully of the superior oblique muscle is attached, may be distinguished. The roof of the orbit as well as part of its floor is excessively thin, the former in old persons being sometimes no thicker than writing paper; it may therefore be easily fractured by a comparatively insignificant implement.

Eyelids, etc.—The skin covering the upper eyelid is thin and delicate, loosely attached to the subjacent tissues, fringed at its margin with two or more rows of hairs, the eye-lashes, and marked with several crescentic furrows, convex upwards. Incisions in this part should be made parallel to these lines. The lax attachment of the skin renders the accumulation of fluid in the subcutaneous areolar tissue an easy matter, the large effusion of blood in the common black eye being thus accounted for. This is also a position often selected for the first appearance of puffiness at the commencement of renal anasarca or dropsy.

By pinching up the eyelid in the subject the student

will feel the so-called tarsal cartilage, to the inner end
of which is attached the palpebral ligament or tendo
oculi affixed at its other end to the margin of the orbit.
To find this it is only necessary to close the eyelids
and draw them outwards when the ligament will be
made tense and appear under the skin as a transverse
ridge.   This ridge is an important surgical landmark,
as it crosses the lachrymal sac at the junction of its
upper and middle thirds, and thus serves as a guide to
the surgeon in opening the latter for the evacuation of
an abscess.   The student should place his finger upon
his own tendo, and open and close the eyelids several
times, in order to note that each time the latter occurs
the ligament is made tense.   A sucking action on the
part of the subjacent sac is thus produced, by means of
which the tears are drawn into its interior through the
canaliculi.

Having studied this ligament the student may next
practice eversion of the eyelid, one of those very minor
operations on the deft performance of which so much of
the comfort of a patient depends.   Mr. Nettleship
thus describes it :—" The patient looks down, a probe
is laid along the lid above the upper edge of the
"cartilage," the lashes, or edge of the lid, are then
seized by a finger and thumb of the other hand, and
turned up over the probe which is simultaneously
pushed down.   After a little practice the probe can be
dispensed with, and the lid everted by the forefinger
and thumb of one hand alone, one serving to fix and
depress the lid, the other to turn it upwards."

When the lid is everted the roots of the hairs will be seen under the conjunctiva as well as the Meibomian follicles which appear like rows of yellow granules. It is in these or in connection with the hair follicles that the common styes are formed. The transition of epidermis into conjunctiva at the margin of the lid should be noticed, as also the fornix or cul-de-sac formed by the passage of the palpebral conjunctiva on to the eye. A similar but shallower depression exists in connection with the lower lid. The lid may now be restored to its normal position. At the inner angle or canthus will be noticed a recess bounded by two prominences, the papillæ lachrymales, on each of which opens the minute aperture of the punctum lachrymale, the lower being a little larger and more external. Through these the tears pass by the canaliculi into the lachrymal sac, and thus into the inferior meatus of the nose by the nasal duct. The canaliculi may have to be slit open and a probe passed into this duct, which is a little more than half an inch in length, and is directed downwards and slightly backwards and outwards. Two other structures are to be noticed in connection with the above mentioned recess, the plica semilunaris, a fold of conjunctiva representing the membrana nictitans or third eyelid of birds, and the caruncula lachrymalis, a reddish eminence covered with a few fine hairs and containing in its interior specialised sweat glands and sebaceous glands.

Eyeball.—A description of the eyeball is outside the scope of this book, but the attention of the student

may be drawn to the fact that neither the cornea nor
the pupil are as a rule mathematically circular, the
former having a tendency to be broader transversely.
The pupil is situated very slightly to the inner side of
the iris. The student should take the opportunity of
examining a number of healthy eyes in order to form a
standard in his own mind of the normal tension of
the globe. With respect to this procedure, Nettleship
states :—" The patient looks steadily down and gently
closes the eyelids ; the observer then makes light pressure on the globe through the upper lid, alternately
with a finger of each hand as in trying for fluctuation,
but much more delicately. The finger-tips are placed
very near together, and as far back over the sclerotic
as possible, not over the cornea. The pressure must
be gentle, and be directed vertically *downwards, not
backwards.* It is best for each observer to keep to one
pair of fingers, not to use the index at one time and
the middle finger at another. Patient and observer
should always be in the same relative position, and it
is best for both to stand and face one another. Always
compare the tension of the two eyes. Be sure that the
eye does not roll upwards during examination, for if
this occur a wrong estimate of the tension may be
formed. Some test both eyes at once with two fingers
of each hand." The tension may be increased so that
indentation of the globe is difficult or impossible, or on
the other hand it may be decreased. For the scale
employed in registering these changes, and the conditions in which they occur, the student is referred to
special text-books on the eye.

III. The Nose.

There is not very much to be made out from an anterior inspection of this organ unaided by instruments, and the investigation of its posterior part may be more conveniently deferred to be considered with the cavity of the mouth. It should first be noticed that the apertures of the nostrils are placed at a lower level than the floor of the inferior meatus; in order therefore that this may be seen or that a speculum may be introduced, it will be necessary to raise the tip of the nose, the head being thrown back. The mobility due to the cartilaginous basis of the anterior part of the nose, allows of the tip being raised and of the dilatation of either nostril.

The apertures of the nostrils are generally more or less compressed laterally in the adult, circular in children, and separated from one another by the thickened lower margin of the septum—the columna nasi. On looking into either, the vestibule or dilated anterior part is seen containing coarse hairs—the vibrissæ. The anterior extremity of the inferior turbinated bone can be seen and felt; in the undissected state only about one-twentieth of this consists of bone, the remainder consisting of the erectile tissue of Voltolini and others. The other turbinated bones cannot be seen without the aid of a speculum, which brings into view the middle one; but it is well to remember that they encroach largely upon the space in the posterior part of the organ. In inserting forceps therefore they should be so introduced that the blades may be opened upwards and downwards, not laterally. The septum in a portion of its extent may be seen, the part visible being chiefly cartilaginous; it is often deflected to one side or the other, or sometimes first to one side and then to the other, the so-called sinuous deflection. In 76·9 per cent. of a large number of skulls examined by Morell Mackenzie, the bony septum was more or less asymmetrical. It is placed in the median line until the seventh year (Zuckerkandl and Symington), and the subsequent deflection which is most often to the left is attributed by some writers to the habit of constantly blowing the nose with the same hand. It may be so great as to cause the introduction of instruments to be difficult or even impossible.

In connection with the examination of the nose from the front, the student should practice the operation of introducing the Eustachian catheter. Should the actual instrument not be at hand, one may be improvised from a probe or even a piece of wire of suitable size with a rounded end, either being bent at an angle of 60° a short distance from its extremity. The operator will be much assisted by practising at first upon a head which has been divided by a mesial anterior posterior section, as he will then be able to watch the point of his instrument as he endeavours to introduce it into the opening of the Eustachian tube. Should such a section be unattainable for this purpose, the position of parts should at least be examined in a specimen before the operation is attempted. The directions for performing the operation are thus given by Pritchard:—" The curved end is introduced into one nostril, keeping the beak close along the angle formed by the septum and the floor. By this means the surgeon will avoid getting into the middle meatus, and so finding himself in difficulty further on. When the catheter has passed the posterior nares, it will soon encounter the back of the pharynx, and this will be easily recognised by its tension, for it has been very aptly described as feeling like the outstretched palm of the hand. The catheter should then be withdrawn about half an inch, and the point turned almost directly outwards, after which, on the catheter being again slightly pushed in, the point will enter the Eustachian tube."

When the catheter is engaged in the Eustachian aperture its beak will be found to point towards the outer angle of the orbit on the same side.

IV. The Ear.

The external ear or pinna is formed throughout the greater part of its extent of a cartilaginous substratum, to which, as in the case of the cartilaginous part of the nose, the skin is very closely adherent. The dependent portion, the lobule, alone contains no cartilage, and consists mainly of fat, the amount of its connection with the side of the neck being variable. The plate of

cartilage occupying the remainder of the pinna is
folded so as to present several elevations and depres-
sions, to which designations have been assigned.
Surrounding the entrance to the meatus is the deepest
hollow, the concha, which is prolonged downwards and
forwards into a notch, bounded on either side by a
prominence.   The anterior of these, which bears hairs,
is called the tragus, the posterior the anti-tragus.
Superior and internal to the former the helix commences and passes round the outer border of the ear as
a well-marked fold, which terminates at the posterior
part of the lobule.   It is sometimes possessed of a
pointed process placed on its inner border, and at its
upper and posterior part, which was first noticed by
Woolner, the sculptor, and to which attention was
directed by Darwin in his *"Expression of the Emotions."*

Commencing at the anti-tragus is another elevation,
the anti-helix, which passing round the concha, bifurcates to enclose a triangular depression—the fossa trian-
gularis or fossa of the anti-helix.   Between the two
elevations is a shallow groove—the fossa scaphoidea or
fossa of the helix.   The outer aperture of the external
auditory meatus is largest from above downwards ; it
possesses a number of hairs, and under the skin are
placed the ceruminous or wax-producing glands.

The canal of the meatus passes forwards in its entire
course.   Its outer portion also passes upwards and
its inner downwards.   In order to obtain a view of the
meatus and membrana tympani, either with or without
the aid of a speculum, it is necessary to straighten the

canal as far as possible. This is done by taking hold of the pinna above and pulling it upwards and slightly backwards and outwards.

V. The Mouth.

The cavity of the mouth may be divided into two parts. One between the lips and cheeks and the teeth—the vestibulum oris, and a second behind the teeth—the cavum oris. Still further back behind the pillars of the fauces is the upper part of the pharynx. In the vestibule there may be felt with the tip of the tongue in one's own mouth or with the fingers in another person's, a number of small granules under the mucous membrane. These are mucous glands, which may, in certain conditions, become chronically hypertrophied or otherwise diseased. On the inner side of the cheek the aperture of the duct of Steno should be sought. This opening, which is much smaller than the calibre of the canal which it terminates, is placed opposite the corner of the second upper molar tooth and is surrounded by a group of small glands, the so-called " molar-glands."

It may be found in the living subject by everting the cheek and wiping the inner surface dry, when in a short time the appearance of a drop of saliva will indicate the opening. If the upper lip be everted a fold of mucous membrane—the frænum labii superioris, will be seen passing from it to the gums. A finger should be passed up between the cheek and the teeth and the coronoid process felt from within the mouth. The spot above the second bicuspid tooth, where the antrum is sometimes tapped, should also be noticed. Without pausing to describe the teeth, an account of which must be sought in the ordinary text-books, we may pass to the cavum oris situated behind them. The tongue with its filiform and fungiform papillæ is the first object for inspection ; a good idea of the distribution of the last mentioned papillæ will be gained by looking at them in a patient suffering from scarlet fever. At the posterior part will be seen the large circumvallate papillæ, seven to twelve in number, arranged in the form of a V, with the apex directed backwards, and the foramen cæcum situated just behind. If the tongue be pulled well out and to one side the student will see in front of the anterior pillar of the fauces on the bower of the tongue, an area with a few, generally five, longitudinal folds—the papilla foliata.

A finger should now be introduced gradually backwards in the middle line, and the various structures met with investigated. Immediately behind the centre of the root of the tongue, a ridge of mucous membrane will be felt passing to the epiglottis. This is the glosso-epiglottic fold or frænum epiglottidis, on each side of which there is a shallow depression in which a foreign body may lodge. Behind this fold is the epiglottis itself, which may be distinctly felt and even seen in some individuals if the tongue is pulled well out in the middle line. Passing over the epiglottis the finger reaches the ary-epiglottic folds of mucous membrane with the entrance to the larynx between. On each side will be felt the hyoid space, another favourite spot for the lodgment of foreign bodies, and the great cornu of the hyoid bone.

In the middle line the cricoid, as far down as its lower border, can be made out, together with the commencement of the œsophagus. As this spot is one of the two narrowest parts of the gullet, insufficiently masticated lumps of meat and other bodies are liable to lodge in it. The posterior wall of the pharynx overlying the vertebral column may be investigated in its entire extent, and a bulging which may indicate post pharyngeal abscess discovered. In the course of these observations the students should consider their bearing upon the passing of an œsophageal tube or bougie, and in either case the end of the instrument should be kept well against the posterior wall in order to avoid any danger of its entering the larynx by mistake.

The tip of the tongue should now be turned upwards, when the large ranine veins will be distinctly seen on the under surface of the organ. Two fringes of fimbriated mucous membrane which indicated the position of the more deeply seated ranine arteries, will also be noticed. Passing from the tongue to the floor of the mouth is a fold of mucous membrane, the frænum linguæ, sometimes abnormally short, and then causing the condition known as "tongue-tie." On each side of this a duct of Wharton opens on a papilla in the floor of the mouth. If one forefinger be pressed

upwards and inwards from without, beneath the angle
of the jaw, and the other be placed in a corresponding
position under the tongue, the sub-maxillary gland will
be felt between the two under the floor of the mouth.
A long ridge of mucous membrane on either side of the
floor contains the sublingual gland, and indicates to a
certain extent the direction of Wharton's duct and the
lingual nerve. Upon this ridge open, by a number of
apertures, such of the ducts of the last mentioned gland
as do not join the Whartonian canal. Finally, so far
as this part is concerned, the attachment of the genio-
hyo-glossi muscles may be felt under the floor of the
mouth, immediately behind the symphisis of the lower
jaw.

The tongue being restored to its place, the student
should examine the hard palate, the shape of the arch
of which varies in different subjects, being most pointed
and arch-like it is said in congenital idiots. The
mucous membrane is very firmly adherent to the bones
which it covers; under it on either side at the posterior
part may be felt the pulsations of the posterior palatine
artery. The canal through which this vessel passes to
reach the palate is placed just internal to the last
molar tooth, and may be plugged for the arrest of
hæmorrhage. Carry the finger a little further back
and the point of the hamular process of the pterygoid
plate, as well as that structure itself, and the pterygoid
fossa may all be felt, together with the back of the
antrum and the external pterygoid plate behind the
last molar. The pterygo-maxillary ligament may be

seen and felt when the mouth is widely opened, extending from the internal pterygoid plate to the lower
jaw behind the last molar, and separating the buccinator from the superior constrictor. This ligament
helps us to find the position of the gustatory nerve,
which lies a little below it, on the bone below the last
molar tooth. It is here that the nerve is sometimes
divided for the relief of painful cancer of the tongue.
The guides for the division of two other nerves in the
cavity of the mouth may also here be mentioned. The
inferior dental nerve is reached by an incision "from
the last upper molar to the last lower molar, just to
the inner side of the anterior border of the coronoid
process. The cut passes through the mucous membrane down to the tendon of the temporal muscle.
The finger is introduced into the incision, and passed
between the ramus of the jaw and the internal
pterygoid muscle, until the bony point is felt that
marks the orifice of the dental canal. The nerve is
here picked up with a hook, isolated and divided."
(Treves).

The buccal nerve which is sometimes divided for
neuralgia is thus reached: "the surgeon places the
finger nail upon the outer lip of the anterior border of
the ascending ramus of the lower jaw at its centre, and
divides in front of this border the mucous membrane
and the fibres of the buccinator vertically. He then
seeks for the nerve, separating the tissues with a director,
and divides it." (Stimson).

The student should now examine the structures,

separating the cavity of the mouth from the pharynx, the soft palate with its central dependance, the uvula, the folds of mucous membrane covering the palato-glossus and palato-pharyngeus, and forming the anterior and posterior pillars of the fauces, and the tonsil lying between them. This latter should not project under normal circumstances into the isthmus faucium, and a consideration of its inter-muscular position will explain the great pain caused in swallowing when it is enlarged, and especially when ulcerated also, as in "hospital sore-throat."

The head being thrown well back the posterior nares should be thoroughly explored. By hooking the finger round the soft palate the posterior part of the septum and of the inferior turbinated bone may be felt. If the finger be pushed onwards into the inferior meatus, and the little finger of the other hand be introduced from the front into the same, the two may be made to meet without difficulty unless the passage is abnormally constricted. The apertures of the posterior nares measure a little less than an inch vertically, and half an inch transversely. An investigation of this part will be useful in assisting the student to understand the operation of plugging the posterior nares.

CHAPTER II.

THE SCALP.

I. The Scalp.

For purposes of convenience the scalp is here limited to the part of the head normally clad with hair. The skin and subjacent tissues are here closely united to one another so as to form a dense and thick covering to the cranium. Free movement is permitted, however, between the scalp and the bone beneath it, by the layer of loose connective tissue which lies between the aponeurosis of the occipito-frontalis muscle and the pericranium. The supra-orbital, frontal, and two branches of the superficial temporal artery, have already been alluded to. Behind the ear and over the mastoid process, the pulsations of the posterior auricular artery may be felt; the occipital artery will be found near the centre of a line drawn from the apex of the mastoid process to the external occipital protuberance. A lymphatic gland, the sub-occipital, which receives the lymphatics of the occipital and posterior parietal region, lies a short distance behind the mastoid process, and may be felt when enlarged, a condition which occurs in syphilis and in skin diseases of this region of the scalp.

II. Relation to Bony Vault.

Comparatively few bony points are to be felt through the scalp, yet by means of a few measurements and rules, the positions of the various sutures may be mapped out with considerable accuracy. The bony points which may be felt are the external occipital protuberance at the back of the head, with a portion of

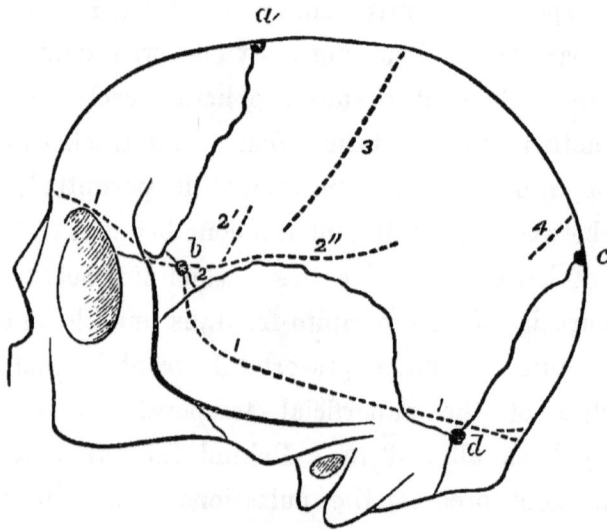

Fig. 2.—Diagram of Cranium.

a. Bregma. *b.* Pterion. *c.* Lambda. *d.* Asterion. 1, 1, 1, Base line of cerebrum. 2 Main portion, 2′ ascending limb, 2″ posterior limb of the fissure of Sylvius. 3. Fissure of Rolando. 4. Parieto-occipital fissure.

the superior curved line passing from it; above the former the apex of the occipital bone may often be distinguished. The mastoid process can be distinctly felt behind the ear, and is a valuable landmark; it is much smaller in the child than in the adult, from the non-development of the air-cells in its interior.

The following points are valuable in mapping out the sutures :—

1. The bregma, or junction of the coronal, sagittal, and in the young subject, frontal sutures ; this is placed at the centre of a line drawn across the vertex from one external auditory meatus to the other, the head being in the usual erect position.

2. The pterion, or junction of the frontal, temporal, parietal and sphenoid bones in the zygomatic fossa. This is generally shaped like an H, of which the anterior limb is formed by the fronto-parietal and sphenoid sutures, the posterior by the temporo-parietal and sphenoid, and the cross-bar by the parieto-sphenoid. The relations of the four bones to one another vary considerably, however, but we may take the cross-bar as being about half an inch in length in the majority of cases. The pterion is situated a little above a line drawn backwards from the external angular process, and from $1\frac{1}{4}$ to $1\frac{1}{2}$ inches posterior to that point.

3. The lambda or junction of the coronal and lambdoidal sutures is situated about $2\frac{3}{4}$ inches above the external occipital prominence, and may often be felt through the scalp.

4. The asterion is the point of junction of the lambdoid and squamous sutures ; it is placed about $\frac{3}{4}$ of an inch behind and $\frac{1}{2}$ an inch above the superior part of the posterior border of the mastoid process.

With the aid of these points we may indicate on

the scalp the position of the sutures of the vault as follows :—

Sagittal extends from the bregma to the lambda.

Coronal extends from the bregma downwards and forwards, past the anterior end of the pterion to just behind and below the external angular process.

Lambdoidal extends from the lambda, past the asterion, and forwards internal to the mastoid process.

Squamous may be indicated by drawing a curved line from the posterior part of the pterion to the asterion, the highest part of which is about two inches above the zygoma.

III. Relation to Membranes of Brain and their Vessels.

The falx cerebri extends from the root of the nose along the frontal and coronal sutures to the external occipital protuberance, and the falx cerebelli is continued down in the middle line to the posterior margin of the foramen magnum. The tentorium so far as it is related to the cranial wall, will be indicated by a line from the external occipital protuberance to the asterion.

The middle meningeal artery lies near the posterior part of the pterion.

The torcular herophili, or posterior point of confluence of the venous sinuses, corresponds nearly to the external occipital protuberance; a line therefore from this point to the root of the nose will indicate the position of the superior longitudinal sinus, one from the former point downwards, that of the occipital, and a third from the same point to the asterion, a part of the lateral.   At the asterion this last sinus turns downwards, and runs behind the posterior border of the mastoid process to the base of the skull.   In this part of its course it is not unfrequently joined by a large vein passing from the scalp through the mastoid foramen.

IV. Fontanelles.

The student should examine the shape and position of the fontanelles in the head of a young infant.   These are spots where the bony vault is incomplete, and where membrane alone underlies the scalp.   The two most important, from the assistance they lend to the obstetrician, in diagnosing the position of the descending head of the child in parturition, as well as from their diagnostic value during infancy, are the anterior and posterior.   The former is diamond-shaped, occupies the position of the bregma, and is included between the two frontal and two parietal bones.   The latter is triangular with its apex directed forwards, it occupies the position of the lambda and is included between the parietal and occipital bones.

V. RELATION OF CRANIUM TO BRAIN.

Although it is much more important for the student
to be acquainted with the relations of the different
parts of the brain to the scalp, a subject to be dealt
with in the next section, their position in connection
with certain of the bony points mentioned in Section
III. may here be mentioned.

The level of the base of the brain may thus be
indicated; a line across the upper margin of the two
supra-ciliary ridges to the pterion gives the lower level
of the frontal lobes, another curved slightly downwards
from the pterion to the asterion, that of the temporo-
sphenoidal, and a third from the asterion to the external
occipital protuberance, marks the line of division between the occipital and posterior part of the tempero-
sphenoidal lobes above, and the cerebellum below the
tentorium.

The fissure of Sylvius commences at the pterion, its
anterior limb runs upwards a short distance behind,
and not quite parallel to, the coronal suture, its posterior lies along the anterior part of the squamous
suture, and where that turns down to pass to the
asterion, continues backwards and upwards across the
parietal bone. The fissure of Rolando commences a
little less than two inches posterior to the bregma and
a short distance from the middle line, and passes down
towards the squamous suture, gradually approaching

the coronal so as to be about three quarters of an inch nearer to it below than above. The parieto-occipital fissure lies a short distance anterior to the external occipital protuberance. It should be mentioned that Symington has shown that in the child the fissure of Sylvius lies half an inch or more above the squamous suture, and that the fissure of Rolando lies farther forward than in the adult.

VI. Relation of Scalp to Brain.

The increasing importance of brain surgery makes the comprehension of the relation between the scalp and the brain a subject of the highest interest to the surgeon. The method here given is that originally described by Dr. R. W. Reid, and justly valued on account of its simplicity and accuracy.

The *longitudinal* fissure is indicated by a line drawn from the glabella to the external occipital protuberance.

The *transverse* fissure is indicated by a line drawn from the external auditory meatus to the external occipital protuberance.

The *fissure of Sylvius* is found by taking a point an inch and a quarter posterior to the external angular process of the frontal, and drawing a line from thence to a point three quarters of an inch below the most prominent part of the parietal eminence. Measured from before backwards, the first three-quarters of an inch represent the main fissure, and the remainder the posterior limb. The anterior limb starts two inches behind the external angular process and runs vertically upwards for about an inch.

The *parieto-occipital fissure* is found by continuing the line of the posterior limb of the fissure of Sylvius to that of the longitudinal fissure, the posterior inch of the line thus formed will approximately indicate the fissure in question.

To find the *fissure of Rolando*, it will be necessary to erect a kind of scaffold formed of three lines. The first or base runs through the lowest part of the infra-orbital margin and the middle of the external auditory meatus. Upon this line are erected two perpendiculars, one starting from the hollow in front of the external auditory meatus, the other from the posterior border of the mastoid process at its root. These three lines taken in conjunction with that for the longitudinal fissure, will enclose a quadrilateral space, and if a diagonal line be drawn from the posterior superior corner to the anterior inferior, it will lie over the fissure of Rolando. To indicate the exact extent of this fissure, a short portion of the line must be omitted above and below, since it is very rare for the fissure of Rolando to pass either into the longitudinal fissure or into that of Sylvius.

The student has thus been enabled to map out on the scalp the great fissures of the brain, and having fully mastered the method pursued, he should next proceed to fill in the smaller details as directed by Dr. Reid.

The *frontal lobe* is bounded above by the line for the longitudinal fissure, below by the line for the trunk and horizontal limb of the Sylvian fissure, behind by the line for the fissure of Rolando, and in front by a line just above and parallel with the supra-orbital margin. A line drawn from the supra-orbital notch backwards to within three-quarters of an inch of the line for the fissure of Rolando, and parallel with the line for the longitudinal fissure, will indicate the first frontal fissure. The frontal part of the temporal ridge will indicate the second frontal fissure. The first, second, and third frontal convolutions, will thus be mapped out. The ascending frontal convolution will occupy a space about three-quarters of an inch broad, parallel with, and in front of, the line for the fissure of Rolando.

The *parietal lobe* will be marked out by the line for the longitudinal fissure superiorly, and in front and behind by the lines for the fissure of Rolando and the parieto-occipital fissure respectively. Below, the line for the horizontal limb of the fissure of Sylvius will separate it from the temporo-sphenoidal lobe. The interval between the posterior end of the Sylvian line and the outer end of the parieto-occipital line is occupied by the junction of the postero-parietal lobule (*p. p. l.*, fig. 4) with the first annectant convolution, and the angular gyrus (*ang. g.*, fig. 4) with the second annectant convolution, the arrangement of these convolutions with regard to one another being very variable, the angular gyrus usually projecting somewhat more posteriorly than the postero-parietal lobule. We can, therefore, only indicate the separation of this part of the parietal lobe from the neighbouring temporo-sphenoidal and occipital lobes by drawing a line (*a*, fig. 4) slightly convex downwards from the posterior end of the Sylvian line to the outer end of the

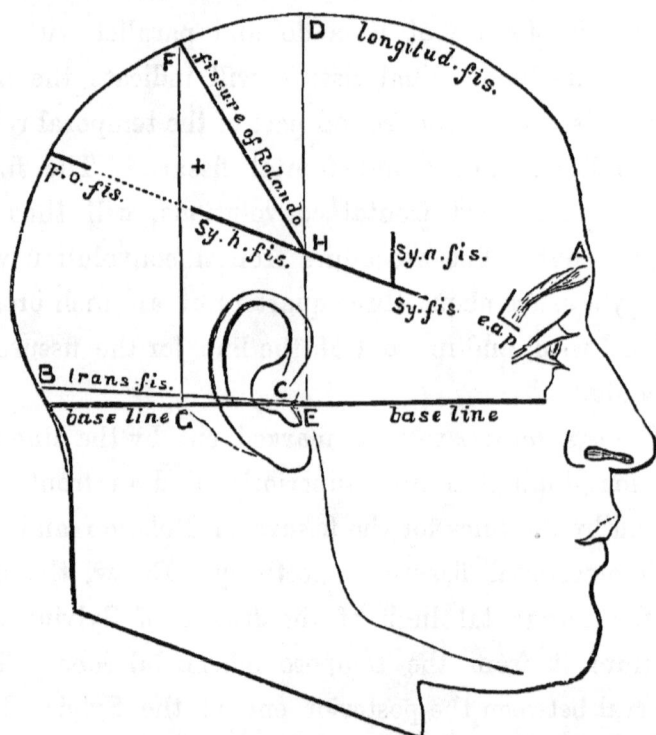

Fig. 3.—Showing Relation of Chief Fissures to Scalp. (Reid).

A. Glabella. *B.* External occipital protuberance. *e. a. p.* External angular process of frontal. *B. C.* Transverse fissure. *A. B.* Horizontal fissure. *Sy. fis.* Sylvian fissure. *Sy. h. fis.* Posterior limb of Sylvian fissure. *Sy. a. fis.* Anterior limb of Sylvian fissure. *DE, FG.* Perpendiculars alluded to in text. *F. H.* Fissure of Rolando. *p. o. fis.* Parieto-occipital fissure. + Most prominent part of parietal eminence parieto-occipital line. An irregularly triangular space will thus be marked out to indicate the parietal lobe. If in this space we draw a line from a point half an inch outside the outer extremity of the parieto-occipital line to a point about an inch above and behind the anterior and inferior angle of the space, this line will lie over the *intra-parietal fissure* (*i. par. f.*, fig. 4). The line must be curved, with its convexity directed forwards and inwards, and parallel in its anterior third or so with the line for the fissure of Rolando, and about three-fourths of an inch behind it. In the space above the intra-parietal sulcus we shall have, in front, parallel with the whole length of the fissure of Rolando, the ascending parietal convolution, and behind, the postero-parietal lobule. The space below the sulcus will indicate, in its anterior part, the supra-marginal convolution (*s. m. c.*, fig. 4) filling up the most prominent part of the parietal eminence, and in its posterior part, the angular gyrus (*ang. g.*, fig. 4).

The *temporo-sphenoidal lobe* is, like the last, somewhat difficult to indicate posteriorly, because it becomes continuous there with the parietal and occipital lobes without any distinct line of demarcation. Its outline will lie in the lower part of the temporal region, extending a little beyond the temporal ridge behind. It will be bounded above by the line of the main trunk and horizontal limb of the fissure of Sylvius, below by the upper border of the zygoma and a line carried back from the posterior end of that to a point midway between the external occipital protuberance, and the

posterior border of the mastoid process at its root.
The anterior border or apex of the lobe will extend as
far forwards as the posterior superior border of the
malar bone.   Behind, the lobe will be bounded by a

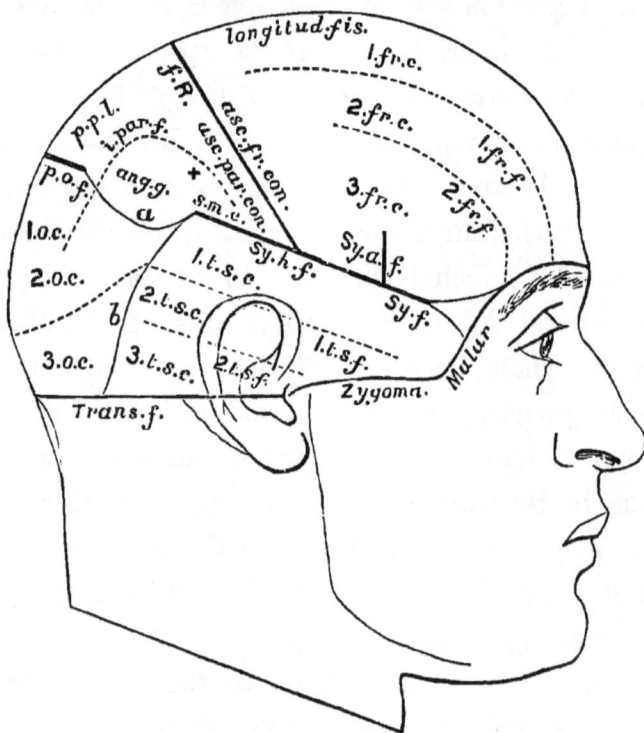

FIG. 4.—SHOWING RELATION OF FISSURES AND CONVOLUTIONS OF
BRAIN TO SCALP. (REID).

+ Most prominent part of parietal eminence.   *a.* Convex line
bounding parietal lobe below.   *b.* Convex line bounding temporo-
sphenoidal lobe behind. 1 *fr. c.* First frontal convolution. 1 *fr. f.*
First frontal fissure. *f. R.* Fissure of Rolando. *Sy. f.* Sylvian fissure. *Sy. h. f.* Horizontal limb of Sylvian fissure. *Sy. a. f.* Ascending limb of Sylvian fissure. *p. o. f.* Parieto-occipital fissure.
i. par. f. Intra-parietal fissure. *ang. g.* Angular gyrus. *s. m. c.*
Supra-marginal convolution. 1 *t. s. c.* First temporo-sphenoidal
convolution. 1 *t. s. f.* First temporo-sphenoidal fissure. 1 *o. c.*
First occipital convolution. *p. p. l.* Postero-parietal lobule.

slightly convex line (*b.*, fig. 4) with the convexity directed backwards, extending from the posterior end of the Sylvian line to the posterior end of the line indicating the lower boundary of the lobe.

A line running about an inch below and parallel with the line for the main trunk and horizontal ramus of the fissure of Sylvius, will indicate the first temporo-sphenoidal fissure (*1 t. s. f.*, fig. 4) and another line about three quarters of an inch below and parallel with the last, will indicate the second temporo-sphenoidal fissure (*2 t. s. f.*, fig. 4). Thus, the first, second, and third temporo-sphenoidal convolutions will be mapped out (*1 t. s. c., 2 t. s. c., 3 t. s. c.*, fig. 4).

The *occipital lobe* will occupy the remaining surface of the scalp. It will be bounded above by the parietal lobe, below by the superior curved line in its inner half, that is, the part of the line unoccupied by the lower limit of the temporo-sphenoidal lobe. Internally, the line of the longitudinal fissure, and externally, the convex line for the posterior border of the temporo-sphenoidal lobe, will bound it. The area of the lobe being marked out, the first, second, and third occipital convolutions, can be readily filled in (*1 o. c., 2 o. c., 3 o. c.*, fig. 4). The student will find a dissection based on this method, for exposing the ascending frontal convolution, which may serve as a model for the exposure of other convolutions, in the second edition of Carrington and Lane's *Manual of Dissections*.

CHAPTER III.

THE NECK.

In this section only the anterior and lateral portions of the neck will be dealt with, the posterior being included with the back.

The skin of the neck is loose and mobile, and is underlaid by a thin layer of muscle passing from the clavicle to cross the lower jaw. This is the platysma myoides, and its fibres run from above downwards and backwards. A great number of structures, many of which are of the highest surgical importance, lie in the region now under consideration, they will be dealt with in the following order:—those in the middle line, between that line and the anterior border of the sterno-mastoid, and those behind that muscle.

I. The Middle Line of the Neck.

The first structure which can be felt beneath the lower jaw is the hyoid bone, the body and great cornua of which can be distinguished. The student in seeking for this should not stretch the tissues of the neck, but should allow the chin to fall and push his finger and thumb up underneath it, when the object of his search will readily be discovered. In the normal position this bone corresponds to the fourth cervical vertebra. Be-

neath it is a space which overlies the anterior thyro-
hyoid membrane, behind which lies the apex of the
epiglottis. The next structure met with is the thyroid
cartilage, or Adam's apple, the largest and most
prominent hard body in the neck, of greater size and
prominence proportionally in men than in women.
The upper border with its notch and superior cornua,
the angle, lower border and inferior cornua by the side
of the cricoid, can all be distinguished. The middle of
the angle corresponds to the attachment of the vocal
cords. Beneath the thyroid cartilage lies the crico-
thyroid membrane, which is divided in laryngotomy,
and on which lie the crico-thyroid branches of the
superior thyroid arteries. The student will note that
these are the first vessels met with in the middle line,
and they are of small size ; incisions for the relief of
cellulitis of the neck may therefore be made in this
line without fear of wounding any vessel of importance.

Below this membrane lies the cricoid cartilage, a
surgical landmark of much importance, which corresponds with the disk between the fifth and sixth
cervical vertebræ. At the lower border of this cartilage the pharynx ends, and the œsophagus commences,
this point being, as has already been mentioned, one of
the narrowest parts of that canal. Below the cricoid
we reach the trachea, about eight of the rings of which
lie above the sternum in the ordinary position, none of
which can, however, be felt as separate structures.
According to Holden only $1\frac{1}{2}$ inches of trachea lie
above the sternum, though an additional $\frac{3}{4}$ inch may

be gained by stretching the neck, but Tillaux gives
somewhat different figures. He states that in a child
from three to five years there is $1\frac{1}{2}$ inches, from six to
seven 2, from eight to ten $2\frac{1}{4}$, and in the normal adult
$2\frac{3}{4}$, the head being in the ordinary position. In the
operation of tracheotomy this tube is opened, in that
of laryngo-tracheotomy its upper rings and the cricoid
cartilage being divided. On account of these operations, and especially the former, which is by far the
commoner, it is very important to know what structures lie in front of the trachea before it enters the
thorax. The first in order from above downwards is
a transverse communicating branch between the two
superior thyroid veins, which is generally present, and
lies over the first ring of the trachea. Next in order is
the isthmus of the thyroid, which varies in size, but
usually overlies the second, third, and fourth rings.
According to Treves the importance of avoiding the
wounding of this structure is overated, and, as he
points out, it has been shown that an injection will
not cross the isthmus from one lobe of the thyroid to
the other. Over the isthmus is a plexus of veins, and
below it they unite into one or generally more inferior
thyroid veins. In this position also is the thyroidea ima
artery when such a vessel exists. At the root of the
neck the trachea recedes considerably from the surface,
a depth of an inch and a half intervening between it
and the skin at the episternal notch. Just above this
last is a transverse trunk uniting the two anterior
jugular veins, which may themselves lie in front of the

trachea, though as a general rule they are some little distance from the middle line. In children, up to the age of two, the thymus gland covers the trachea for a variable distance above the sternum, and the in-nominate artery may also be in that high position, a position which it may retain, though rarely in the adult also. Behind the trachea lies the œsophagus, which in this part of the neck lies slightly to the left side. In feeling for a hard foreign body the attempt should be made on the left side by the trachea, and here also the operation of œsophagotomy is performed.

II. Parts near Anterior Border of Sterno-Mastoid.

The student should first note the exact line of the anterior border of the sterno-mastoid muscle, as he is apt to obtain an incorrect idea of it, from an examination made in the dissected condition. When in an undisturbed condition it does not run a straight course from the sternum to the mastoid process, as it appears to do when its fascial connections have been cut. On the contrary its anterior border passes practically to the angle of the jaw, and is held there by its relations with the cervical fascia. It follows from this that the common carotid artery and its divisions, the external and internal carotids are completely covered in by the anterior border of the muscle in the undissected state. The muscle below arises by two heads, sternal and clavicular, between which a triangular space of variable size is included. At its base lies the line of the sterno-

clavicular joint.   If a needle be pushed in here on
the right side, it will pass immediately above the innominate artery at its bifurcation, and will have below
it and to the right the subclavian artery, external to it
the internal jugular vein, and internal to it the common
carotid artery.   Sometimes in children, and even in
adults, the innominate artery, as has been already
mentioned, rises higher than the sternum, in which
case a needle so introduced would pierce it.

A needle thrust through in a similar position on the
left side would pierce the common carotid artery, and
possibly the internal jugular vein.

The relations of these vessels to the lower end of the
sterno-mastoid should be borne in mind, since it is sometimes necessary for the relief of wry-neck to divide some
part of the muscle in that position.   At the upper part of
the anterior border, if a line be drawn from the hyoid to
the mastoid process, it will correspond to the posterior
belly of the digastric muscle.   Above this lies that
portion of the sub-maxillary gland, which is not deeply
placed behind the jaw, and on its surface are some
lymphatic glands, which are perceptible when enlarged.
Farther down is the lateral lobe of the thyroid body,
which cannot be distinctly made out save when enlarged, but which lies beside the inferior part of the
thyroid cartilage, the cricoid, and the upper five or six
rings of the trachea.

Two veins are related to the external surface of the
sterno-mastoid, viz., the anterior jugular, which runs
downwards along its anterior border, and the external

jugular, which commencing at a point near the angle
of the jaw crosses the muscle and terminates in the
posterior angle at the middle of the clavicle. This
latter vein can be made prominent by pressure applied
at its lower extremity.

The most important structures in the region now
under consideration are the carotid arteries, common,
external and internal, with the branches of the second
named vessel. A line from the sternal extremity of
the clavicle to a point midway between the angle of the
jaw and the mastoid process, indicates the position of
the common carotid. It bifurcates as a rule on a line
with the upper border of the thyroid cartilage. If a
line be drawn downwards and outwards from the
anterior part of the hyoid bone, so as to cross the line
of the carotid at the level of the cricoid cartilage, it
will indicate the position of the anterior belly of the
omo-hyoid muscle. The cricoid cartilage is the guide
for the incisions which are made along the anterior
border of the sterno-mastoid muscle in ligature of the
common carotid. This operation is performed either
above or below the omo-hyoid; in the former case the
centre of the incision is at the level of the cricoid,
in the latter its upper extremity. At the level of
the cricoid cartilage the carotid can be compressed
against the vertebral column, and here also by deep
pressure can be felt the anterior tubercle of the
transverse process of the sixth cervical vertebra, which
is called the "carotid tubercle," and used sometimes
as a guide in the operations mentioned above. It may

also be used as a landmark in tying the vertebral artery. The internal jugular vein lies external to the artery, and the pneumogastric and sympathetic nerves posterior. As regards the branches of the artery, the superior thyroid comes off just below the great cornu of the hyoid, and curves downwards towards the lateral lobe of the thyroid body on the anterior surface of the upper portion of which it may be felt pulsating.

The lingual lies immediately above the great cornu of the hyoid, having above it the lingual nerve and the tendon of the digastric muscle. The facial arises immediately above the lingual, sometimes indeed by a common trunk with the latter, and passes under the jaw in the sub-maxillary gland; it emerges again and crosses the jaw in front of the masseter muscle. The occipital artery may be represented by a line starting from the carotid line just above the level of the great cornu of the hyoid, and passing backwards and upwards so as to cross the mastoid process, beneath which the vessel lies, about a quarter of an inch above its apex.

III. STRUCTURES POSTERIOR TO STERNO-MASTOID.

Behind the sterno-mastoid lies the posterior triangle of the neck, bounded behind by the anterior border of the trapezius, passing from the occiput to the point of the shoulder.

The lower portion of this triangle, separated from the remainder by the posterior belly of the omo-hyoid muscle, is surgically the most important part of the region, and is called the sub-clavian or supra-clavicular triangle. The belly of the muscle just alluded to may be seen in a thin neck after swallowing, when its contraction assists to depress the hyoid; it may also be seen in a person sobbing. It lies nearly parallel with the clavicle, and so short a distance above it that its inferior border is often beneath the edge of that bone, especially if the point of the shoulder is raised. It is only when the shoulder is depressed, and after the skin, fasciæ, and other superficial structures have been removed, that any very distinct triangle therefore exists.

The most important structure in the triangle is the subclavian artery, which there rises about half an inch above the clavicle, so that if a segment of a circle be described of that height, with one cornu at the sternal end and the other at the middle of the clavicle, it will correspond fairly to the position of the artery. Its vein lies on a plane anterior, but under cover of the clavicle. If the student stand behind a living subject, and press his finger or thumb behind the posterior border of the sterno-mastoid, downwards and a little inwards, he will feel the pulsations of the vessel, and can compress it against the first rib. The posterior border of the sterno-mastoid corresponds fairly to the outer border of the scalenus anticus lying under it, and is a guide to the surgeon in tying the artery. If pressure be made backwards and inwards a little above the artery, the transverse process of the seventh cervical vertebra will be felt. The transverse cervical artery may be felt as a rule running a short distance above the clavicle and parallel to it. The cords of the brachial plexus may be felt and even seen in a suitable subject, especially if the arm be pulled down and the head drawn to the opposite side. The outer edge corresponds to a line drawn from a point a little above the cricoid cartilage to one a little external to the centre of the clavicle. The apex of the lung also reaches up into the neck in this position, a fact which should be borne in mind, since this portion is liable to be first attacked in phthisis. The sub-clavian artery arches over it, being only separated from the lung by the dome of the pleura and the fascia covering it. The lung extends into the neck for a distance varying from 1¼ to 2 inches, being higher according to some observers on the right than on the left side. Eichorst, however, says that the apices are almost without exception, placed at the same height. It is safe to conclude that if one side is higher than the other, it will almost certainly be the right.

At the upper part of the posterior triangle, indeed strictly speaking, in front of the triangle and under cover of the sterno-mastoid, the transverse process of the atlas may be felt just below and in front of the apex of the mastoid process.

Three nerve trunks lying in the upper part of the posterior triangle may be indicated by three lines, each drawn from the central point of the posterior border of the sterno-mastoid. The first line passing transversely across that muscle from behind forwards, will indicate the superficial cervical nerve, the second to the back of the cartilage of tho ear, the great auricular, and the third along tho posterior border of the muscle to the scalp, the small occipital.

CHAPTER IV.

THE THORAX.

In this chapter only the anterior and lateral aspects of the thorax will be considered, the remainder being included in that on the back. It is not necessary here to describe the general shape and structure of the thorax, but the student should note the great difference produced in the skeleton by the removal of the shoulder girdle, and should study the relations of the clavicle to the upper part of the cavity. The right side of the thorax is, as a rule, larger than the left. According to Holden, " of ninety-two persons of the male sex and good constitutions, seventy-one had the right side the larger, eleven the left, ten had both sides equal. The maximum of difference in favour of the right was one inch and a quarter. The measurements were made on a plane with the nipple."

Bony points.—The sternum is of course the first object of study. Its upper border, the episternal notch, in inspiration is on a level with the disk between the second and third dorsal vertebræ, and about two inches anterior to it. If the finger be carried downwards, a prominent ridge or angle will be encountered at the junction of the manubrium and gladiolus. This is called the angulus Ludovici, it marks the part of the sternum where union takes place latest, and is of especial importance as a landmark, since it corresponds to the junction of the second costal cartilages with the sternum, and thus enables us to find the second pair of ribs in a fat subject. This ridge corresponds with the lower border of the fourth dorsal vertebra. At the lower part of the sternum the junction of the manubrium with the xiphoid cartilage will be found, this point corresponding to the ninth dorsal vertebra. It is placed a little below the junction of the seventh pair of costal cartilages with the sternum. Though distinct enough in the skeleton it is difficult to make out accurately the edges of the xiphoid cartilage in the recent condition, on account of the ligaments which pass to it from adjacent structures. Sometimes its apex is curved very distinctly forwards, in which case there is a cup-like depression between it and the end of the manubrium.

On either side of the episternal notch the sternoclavicular articulation will be seen, and the changes produced at this joint, as well as in the position of the clavicle during its movements, should be studied by raising and lowering the arm of the subject.

The student should next direct his attention to the ribs, which can easily be counted in a thin person, but are more difficult to identify where there is much subcutaneous fat. The first can be felt by pressing the finger backwards and downwards under the clavicle, external to its articulation with the sternum. This rib has much less mobility than the others, and its cartilage is more often ossified, this being not uncommonly the

E

case in tolerably old subjects. The second corresponds to the angulus Ludovici. Rules for finding some of the others will be found in the next section, in connection with the muscular and other markings related to the soft parts.

By commencing above and counting downwards behind the posterior axillary line, the student will be able to discover the last two ribs, which from their position are sometimes difficult of detection. The last rib is very variable in length, being in some cases four times longer than in others. It is proportionately smaller in women than in men (Macalister). The importance of the last rib as a landmark will be dealt with in the chapter on the abdomen.

The oblique sweep of the ribs causes the anterior extremity of each to lie on a lower plane than its posterior, thus, the first rib in front corresponds to the fourth behind, the second to the sixth, the third to the seventh, the fourth to the eighth, the fifth to the ninth, the sixth to the tenth, and the seventh to the eleventh. By remembering these facts the student will be able to determine what ribs would be divided in a transverse section at any level. The anterior portions of the intercostal spaces are wider than the posterior, and of the former, the third, second, and first, are the widest, in the order mentioned. The operation of paracentesis thoracis, or tapping the pleura, is generally performed in the sixth interspace, at a point midway between the anterior and posterior axillary lines. Some surgeons recommend that a space higher should be taken on the right side, on account of the fact that the dome of the diaphragm rises higher on that side. The trocar should be inserted immediately above the upper border of the lower rib in the space indicated, since there is thus less danger of wounding the intercostal vessels, which lie under cover of the lower border of each rib, in the position in which the operation is performed.

II. Soft Parts.

One of the most important landmarks in the thorax is the nipple. This lies in the majority of cases in the interspace between the fourth and fifth ribs, and about four inches from the middle of the sternum. It may also lie on the fourth rib, more rarely on the fifth, most rarely in the fifth interspace. It is not unfrequently farther from the middle line on the right side, and may be placed at a higher level.

The female breast covers the thorax from the third to the sixth or seventh rib, and from the edge of the sternum to the anterior border of the axilla, its base being somewhat oval, with its long diameter directed downwards and inwards. The nipple is placed a little below the centre of the gland, and is surrounded by an areola, which is pink in the virgin, dark brown, and dappled with lighter spots in the pregnant woman, and after pregnancy becomes a dingy brown, never returning to the virgin hue. Beneath the clavicle the deltoid muscle and the upper border of the pectoralis major will be seen, with a triangular interval between. If the finger be pressed deeply into this space, the coracoid process will be felt.

If the arm be drawn outwards from the chest the great pectoral will be placed on the stretch, and its lower border will indicate the position of the fifth rib with which it corresponds.

If the arm be drawn up by the side of the head, the digitations of the serratus magnus muscle will be seen in a fairly thin subject. The highest of these which is visible corresponds to the sixth rib, and the two below to the seventh and eighth.

III. Relations of Lungs to Thoracic Wall.

After studying the structures to be seen or felt in the wall of the thorax, the student should turn his attention to the relation of the various important structures which that cavity contains to its exterior. He may first proceed to map out the position of the lungs, which may be done in the following manner. A point should be taken behind the outer border of the sterno-mastoid muscle, and about an inch and a half above the clavicle. From this a line should be drawn, passing on each side through the sterno-clavicular articulation to the centre of the angulus Ludovici. This line will be slightly indented above the clavicle by the notch for the subclavian vessels. From the centre of the angulus Ludovici the borders of the two lungs run downwards, parallel and close to one another, to a point midway between the fourth pair of costal cartilages, where they diverge. The left passes outwards along the fourth rib to the apex beat point, turns downwards, crosses the fifth rib, and again turns for a short distance inwards in the fifth interspace and behind the sixth rib, to form a small tongue-like process, the processus lingualis. The hollow or bay in the lung thus formed corresponds to the part of the heart uncovered by lung, the area of cardiac dulness, hereafter to be more particularly alluded to, and is called the incisura cardiaca. The right lung on the contrary passes downwards to meet the sixth rib at the parasternal line. The level at which the lower border of the lung lies from the last points mentioned, is described in a slightly different manner by various observers, as will be seen by the table below.

	EICHORST AND GERHARDT.	USUAL DESCRIPTION.
Nipple line .	7th rib, upper border .	6th rib, lower border.
Axillary line .	8th ,, lower ,, .	8th ,,
Scapular line .	9th ,, .	10th ,,
Vertebral column	10th dorsal v. trans. proc.	

As a matter of fact the position will vary slightly in different bodies in accordance with diverse conditions.

The sac of the pleura extends farther down than the limits mentioned, as of course also does the edge of the lung in a full inspiration. Thus, at the front of the

chest the reflection of the pleura corresponds to the
seventh rib cartilage, passing from its upper to lie
below its lower border at the nipple line. In the
axillary line it lies at the level of the ninth rib, and
posteriorly at that of the twelfth, or lower if that rib

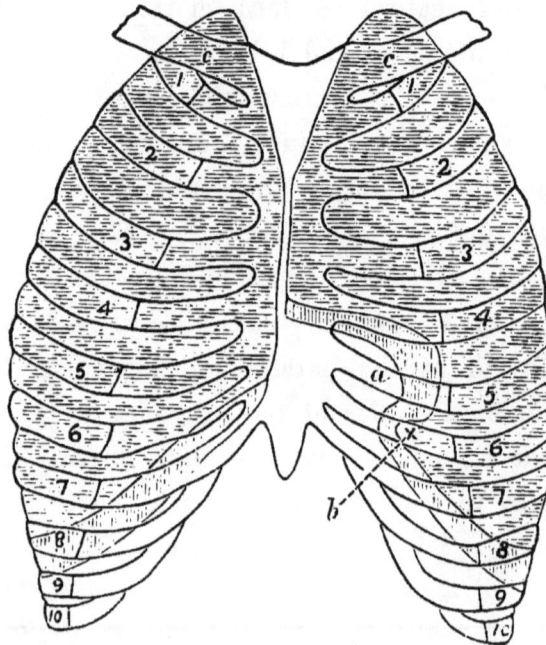

FIG. 5.—DIAGRAM OF RELATION OF LUNGS TO CHEST WALL.

The portion shaded horizontally marks out the area of the lungs,
that shaded vertically the supplementary pleural space. 1-10. Ribs.
c. c. Clavicles. a. Incisura cardiaca. b. Processus lingualis.

be longer than usual. Thus, it is possible for the
pleura and diaphragm to be wounded without the lung
being involved, and also for the diaphragm to be pierced
without any injury to lung or pleura.

The base of the heart corresponds to a line drawn across the sternum at the level of the upper border of the third costal cartilages, which extends half an inch to the right, and about one inch to the left. The right border may be indicated by a curved line drawn from the right extremity of the base to the junction of the seventh right costal cartilage with the sternum; this line will be rather more than $1\frac{1}{2}$ inches from the centre of the sternum at the level of the fourth costal cartilage. The lower border may be indicated by a line drawn from the termination of the last to a point in the fifth interspace, two inches below the nipple, and three and a half from the middle line. The line for the left border runs from the apex in a curve to the left limit of the base. This line will be nearly three inches from the middle point of the sternum at the level of the fourth costal cartilage. The general position of the heart having thus been mapped out it remains to be seen how its various cavities lie. The right auricle forms the major part of the right border, and lies beneath the third, fourth, and fifth costal cartilages, with the intervening spaces and a part of the sternum, the tip of its appendix being placed on the base line at the mid-sternum. The groove between right auricle and ventricle nearly corresponds to a line drawn from the third left costal cartilage at its junction with the sternum, to the sixth right at a similar point. The

left border is formed by the small portion of the left
ventricle, which lies in front, the greater portion of the
anterior surface unaccounted for belonging to the right
ventricle.

The tip of the left auricular appendix lies behind the
lower part of the second left interspace and the upper
part of the third costal cartilage.

The position of the apex-beat is in the fifth interspace
two inches below, and one inch internal to the nipple,
but varies slightly according to the position of the body.
Symington and others have pointed out that in the
infant the heart has a greater breadth in proportion to
the size of the chest than in the adult. Consequently
in children the apex-beat is often below or even external to the nipple line. Steffen believed that it was
pathological if it lay more than $\frac{3}{8}$ of an inch external
to that line. In children the beat may also be in the
fourth interspace, whilst in the aged it may be in the
sixth.

The portion of the heart uncovered by the lungs,
or area of precordial dulness, may be indicated by a
triangle, of which the base is formed by a line drawn
from the apex-beat to a little to the right of the middle
line of the lower end of the gladiolus, and the left side by
a line from the apex to the mid-sternal line at the level
of the fourth pair of costal cartilages. The third side
is formed by joining the upper and lower sternal points.
At the lower angle on the right side the cardiac dulness
shades off into that caused by the liver. The precordial area may also be indicated by Latham's method,

which consists in describing a circle two inches in
diameter, around a point midway between the left
nipple and the end of the gladiolus. This circle is

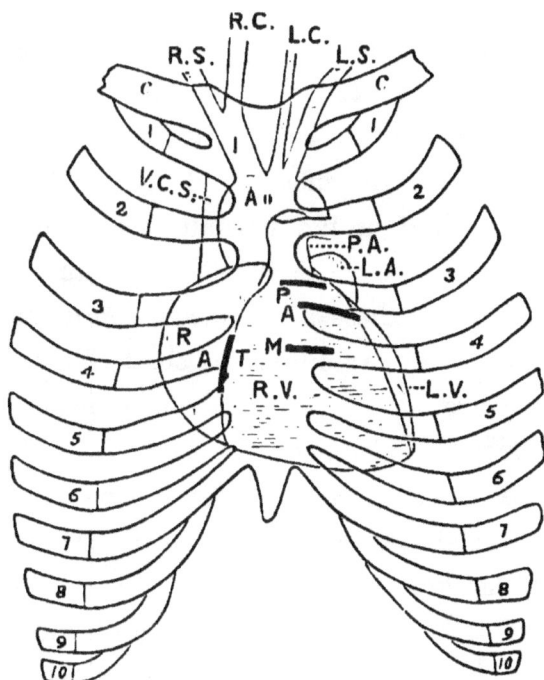

FIG. 6.—DIAGRAM OF RELATION OF HEART AND GREAT VESSELS TO
CHEST WALL (Modified from Quain).

1-10. Ribs. *c. c.* Clavicles. R. V. Right ventricle. L. V. Left
ventricle. R. A. Right auricle. L. A. Left auricle. P. Pulmonary,
A. Aortic, M. Mitral, T. Tricuspid valves. Ao. Aorta. R. I. Innominate artery. R. S. and R. C. Right subclavian and carotid. L. S.
and L. C. Left subclavian and carotid. P. A. Pulmonary artery.
V. C. S. Superior vena cava.

sufficiently accurate for practical purposes. The position of the valves should next be marked out. The
pulmonary orifice lies most superficially, and is placed

to the left of the sternum, and behind it and the third costal cartilage. The aortic valves lie posteriorly and slightly inferiorly to the last, being placed opposite the lower part of the third left cartilage and the third intercostal space. The tricuspid valves lie behind the sternum at the level of the fourth intercostal space and a part of the fourth costal cartilage. The mitral valves, which are the most deeply situated of all, lie under the left half of the sternum and a small portion of the fourth left costal cartilage. The student should bear in mind that these are the *anatomical* positions of the valves, but in examining the chest with the stethoscope, they are not the points at which murmurs at the various orifices are best heard. Murmurs at the aortic orifice are most distinct at the second right costal cartilage, sometimes called the " aortic cartilage " from this fact, those of the pulmonary orifice are heard over the second left interspace close to the sternum, of the mitral at the apex-beat, and of the tricuspid at the ensiform cartilage.

V. Relations of Vessels, etc., to Thoracic Wall.

1. **Aorta.**—The ascending portion of the aortic arch passes from the lower part of the third left costal cartilage to the upper border of the second right, and passes just so far from under cover of the sternum that a needle driven through the second right interspace, close to the sternum, will penetrate the great sinus. The trans-

verse portion crosses behind the sternum just below the middle of the manubrium, a needle driven through at that point passing immediately above it. The end of the transverse and the descending portions form such a curve that a needle, pushed in through the first right interspace beside the sternum, passes under the concavity of the arch close to the ductus arteriosus, and enters the right border of the descending portion deeper in the thorax.

2. **Innominate artery.**—This vessel arises from the arch at the middle of the manubrium, a needle pushed through at this point passing through the left vena innominata, the innominate artery, the trachea and œsophagus, and lodging in the third dorsal vertebra. From the point mentioned it passes upwards, and to the right to terminate behind the right sterno-clavicular articulation, or sometimes a little higher.

3. **Left common carotid.**—This vessel arises from the arch a little to the left of the middle line, and passes to the left sterno-clavicular articulation. To its left again arises the left subclavian artery.

4. **Superior vena cava.**—A needle pushed through the first right interspace, half an inch from the sternum, pierces this vessel at the point of its formation by the junction of the right and left innominate veins. A needle pushed in through the third right interspace, half an inch from the edge of the sternum, pierces the vein where it opens into the right auricle.

5. **Inferior vena cava.**—The opening of this vein into the right auricle lies under the mesial portion of

the fifth right interspace, and the adjacent part of the sternum.

6. **Trachea.**—The trachea bifurcates at or just below the angulus Ludovici, and opposite the fourth dorsal vertebra. The right bronchus lies behind the cartilage of the second right rib at the edge of the vertebral column, and the left behind the second left interspace in a similar position.

7. **Diaphragm.**—In the dead subject the dome of the diaphragm is generally said to rise as high as the fifth rib on the right side, and the sixth on the left. This is of course subject to great variations, according to the period of respiration in the living, and may vary also in the dead. Thus, a needle pushed through at the point of the apex-beat in the fifth interspace at the left side, may pass twice through the diaphragm, wounding the stomach intermediately.

CHAPTER V.

THE ABDOMEN.

In this chapter the anterior part of the abdominal wall alone is considered, together with its relation to the viscera and other structures. The posterior and postero-lateral portions will be dealt with in the chapter on the back, and the perinæum and male and female genitalia form a separate chapter.

I. Bony Prominences.

The xiphoid cartilage and the costal arch have already been alluded to. At the lower part of the abdomen the crest of the ilium and anterior superior spine of the ilium are readily to be distinguished. In the erect posture a line drawn so as to connect the latter prominences on either side, passes a little below the promontory of the sacrum. The symphysis pubis, and on either side of it the pubic spine, should be identified. The former is covered by a pad of fat of considerable size in females, in whom it is called the mons veneris, the term mons jovis being sometimes applied to it in the male. Should any difficulty be found in distinguishing the spine it may be discovered by invaginating the scrotum and pushing the finger up along the cord, or by abducting the leg and tracing upwards the border of the adductor longus muscle. The spine of the pubes is an important landmark in connection with inguinal and femoral herniæ, as it lies inferior and external to the first, and superior and internal to the last. It is nearly in the same horizontal line as the apex of the great trochanter.

II. Skin Markings, etc.

The linea alba forms the middle line of the abdomen, it is the line of junction of the anterior aponeuroses in the interval between the two recti muscles, and though it extends from the xiphoid cartilage to the pubes, is only distinctly marked as a groove above the umbilicus. It is the thinnest and least vascular part of the abdominal wall, for which reasons it is selected usually as the site of the incision in abdominal sections. On each side of it lies the prominence of the rectus muscle, bounded externally by a curved line, the linea semilunaris, which extends from the tip of the ninth or tenth rib to the spine of the pubes. The rectus muscle is intersected by certain horizontal lines, the lineæ transversæ. There are usually three of these, one being placed at the tip of the xiphoid cartilage, a second midway between it and the umbilicus, or on a level with the tenth costal cartilages, and the third at the umbilicus itself. A fourth may be present below the umbilicus. The position of the umbilicus is somewhat variable, but always below a point midway between the xiphoid cartilage and the. symphysis pubis.

It is generally described as corresponding to the disk between the third and fourth lumbar vertebræ, or to the tip of the spinous process of the third lumbar vertebra.

The older writers believed it to be the central point

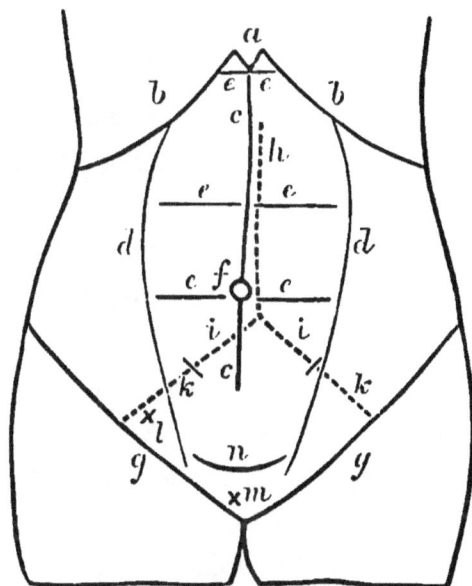

FIG. 7.—DIAGRAM OF ANTERIOR SURFACE OF ABDOMEN.

a. Xiphoid cartilage. *b. b.* Costal arch. *c c.* Linea alba. *d. d.* Lineæ semilunares. *e. e.* L. transversæ. *f.* Umbilicus. *g. g.* Poupart's ligaments. *h.* Abdominal aorta. *i.* Common, *k.* External iliac arteries. *l.* Internal, *m.* External abdominal rings. *n.* Suprapubic fold.

of the body, but this idea is incorrect. According to Mr. Roberts (*Anthropometry*) "at the time of birth, when the child is about the sixth of the height it will ultimately attain to, the point which divides the total height into two equal parts is a little above the navel ;

at two years of age it is at the navel; at three years, when the child has attained half its total height, the central point is on a line with the upper borders of the iliac bones; at ten years of age, when the child has attained three fourths of its total height, the central point is on a line with the trochanters; at thirteen years it is at the pubes, and in the adult man it is nearly half an inch lower. In the adult woman the central point is a little above the pubes."

In fat subjects two lines cross the abdomen transversely, one at the umbilicus and one above the pubes. When the bladder is tapped above the pubes the trochar is passed through the linea alba at the point where it is intersected by the latter.

Poupart's ligament may be seen and felt extending in a gentle curve convex downwards, from the anterior superior spine of the ilium to the spine of the pubes. The external abdominal ring lies just above the crest of the pubes, having the spine external to it. It may be felt by invaginating the scrotum and pushing the finger up in front of the cord.

The internal ring is situated half an inch above the middle point of Poupart's ligament. A line drawn from one ring to the other will indicate the position and limits of the inguinal canal. It should be remembered that in the child at birth there is scarcely any true inguinal canal, as the rings almost overlie one another.

The position of the nerves of the abdomen is of importance in connection with certain forms of vertebral disease which cannot here be particularly considered, and the student should therefore be familiar with their approximate position. The tenth nerve is nearly in a line with the umbilicus, the eighth with the middle linea transversa, the sixth and seventh supply the area above this and between the two limbs of the costal arch. The ilio-hypogastric and ilio-inguinal lie close above Poupart's ligament.

III. Relations of Viscera to the Abdominal Wall.

In the middle line behind the linea alba the disposition of the viscera from above downwards is briefly as follows. Below the xiphoid cartilage lies a part of the left lobe of the liver, beneath which is the stomach. Next comes the transverse colon, then the small intestines, and finally the apex of the bladder, if sufficiently distended. It will now be necessary to consider these and other viscera more particularly.

1. **Stomach.**—This organ, whilst comparatively fixed at its cardiac extremity, is moveable to a considerable extent at its pyloric, and consequently alters in its relations according to the amount of its distension. The cardiac orifice lies about one inch from the sternum behind the seventh left costal cartilage, and corresponds to the spine of the ninth dorsal vertebra posteriorly. The fundus lies to the left of this and on a higher level, rising as high as the upper border of the sixth rib, or even higher, so as to be placed just behind the apex of

the heart. If a line be drawn downwards from the right border of the sternum, and another from the end of the bony portion of the seventh rib, the point at which these intersect will indicate the position of the pylorus in the empty condition of the stomach. But when full the pylorus may move as much as three inches to the right, so as to lie behind the junction of the seventh and eighth right rib cartilages. It is situated on a plane deeper than that of the cardiac opening. A line drawn so as to connect the tips of the seventh costal cartilages will indicate the lower limit of the empty organ; when distended it reaches to a point from $\frac{3}{4}$ to $1\frac{1}{2}$ inches above the umbilicus. In the operation of gastrostomy the incision is generally made parallel to the left side of the costal arch, and about two fingers breadth below it, as the stomach is here uncovered by liver, and in contact with the anterior abdominal wall.

2. **Liver.**—In the erect posture the liver descends about half an inch below the costal arch, though it is a matter of some difficulty to feel it in that position. It is much more obvious beneath the xiphoid cartilage, where in the angle of the costal arch the lower border of the organ may be indicated by a line drawn from the ninth right to the eighth left costal cartilage. The size of the left lobe is somewhat variable, and its left extremity may extend from an inch and a half external to the sternum, or to any point between this and the left mammillary line. Its extent is much greater in the infant. The position of the convex upper surface

varies according to posture, and to the period of respiration at which it is examined. The convex surface on the right side lies beneath the seventh to the eleventh ribs inclusive, and the cartilages of the sixth to the ninth also inclusive. On the left side it does not reach so high a level. Under ordinary circumstances about an inch of the left lobe lies to the right of the middle line, but Symington has recently shown that the left lobe and the anterior surface of the right have a certain amount of mobility, and are displaced slightly to the right when the stomach is distended. The gall bladder has its fundus placed near the surface, by the outer border of the right rectus muscle, and under the ninth right costal cartilage.

3. **Spleen.**—This organ cannot be felt under the edge of the ribs save when pathologically enlarged. It lies beneath the ribs from the eighth or ninth to the eleventh inclusive, and nearly in the line of the posterior part of the tenth. Its mesial extremity is about 1½ inches from the middle line, and its outer about the same distance from the mid-axillary. It should, however, be remembered that it is subject, within physiological limits, to considerable variations in size.

4. **Pancreas.**—It is very rarely possible to feel this organ, but in a very thin subject with flaccid abdominal walls, it may be distinguished. It lies on the vertebral column over the disk between the first and second lumbar vertebræ and the adjacent bodies, and should consequently be sought in the middle line of the ab-

domen, nearly midway between the xiphoid cartilage and the umbilicus.

5. **Intestines.**—Save where it is hidden from the liver and spleen at the hepatic and splenic flexures, the colon is near to the surface, its transverse portion varying in height from the region of the umbilicus or below it, to two inches or so above. When dilated by gas its situation may be ascertained by percussion, and masses of hardened fæces, when present, can be felt in its interior. The site of the cæcum in the right iliac fossa is an important object of investigation in enteric fever, and fæces in constipation may accumulate there or in other parts, especially in the sigmoid flexure, which lies in the left iliac fossa. The small intestine occupies the portion of the abdomen below the transverse colon. Mr. Treves concludes from his laborious investigations, that it is impossible to localise the position of any of the coils connected with the mesentery.

6. **Bladder.**—The bladder cannot be distinguished above the pubes save when distended. In this condition it may extend up to the umbilicus, or to any point between it and the pubic symphysis. In extreme distension from retention of urine, its outline can easily be distinguished, and the fluctuation of its contents felt. It carries the peritoneum before it as it pushes its way upwards, so that an uncovered space of greater or less extent exists, through which the trocar is passed in the operation of tapping above the pubes.

Other points in connection with the colon and the kidneys will be dealt with in the chapter on the back.

IV. Relation of Vessels to the Abdominal Wall.

The abdominal aorta lies on the left side of the vertebral column, and generally divides into the two common iliac arteries opposite the middle of the body of the fourth lumbar vertebra. Its bifurcation is, however, subject to considerable variations.

When it divides at the usual situation it will nearly correspond to a point a little to the left side of the centre of a line drawn so as to connect the highest parts of the two iliac crests. This point will be placed about ¾ of an inch below and to the left of the umbilicus. If two lines be drawn from it, curving slightly outwards, to a point a little internal to the middle either of Poupart's ligament, they will correspond to the common and external iliac arteries. The former of these vessels is somewhat variable in length, but speaking generally, about two inches of either line, or rather more on the right, will correspond to its limits. A line drawn from the point where Poupart's ligament crosses the external iliac to the edge of the rectus, about an inch or more below the umbilicus, will indicate the position of the deep epigastric artery, and the triangle thus included will correspond to Hesselbach's triangle. The cœliac axis corresponds to the twelfth dorsal vertebra behind, and to a point four or five inches above the umbilicus in front. The superior mesenteric artery arises just below this, and the renal arteries an inch lower down. The inferior mesenteric s given off about one inch above the umbilicus.

CHAPTER VI.

THE PERINEUM AND GENITALIA.

I. The Male.

The student should first of all practise the operation of passing the catheter or sound, a procedure more difficult in the dead subject than in the living, when the latter is not affected with a stricture.   The sound should be well oiled, and its passage will be facilitated by dilating the mouth of the urethra and pouring a little oil into it.   The operator should stand on the left side of the body and hold the penis in the left hand.   Stretching the penis he should introduce the instrument, keeping the handle in the line of the left groin at first.   As it glides down the urethra it should gradually be carried towards the middle line, until its direction corresponds with the long axis of the body, from which it should not be allowed to swerve.   When the instrument has been passed a certain distance a slight obstruction will be met with, which is the base of the triangular ligament.   The handle should then be slightly depressed, when a little gentle pressure will carry the point of the instrument into the bladder. If the student finds it difficult to accomplish this he may pass his left forefinger into the rectum and guide the point of the instrument, which will be easily felt, with it. Having passed the sound into the bladder it should bo withdrawn, and the manœuvre repeated several times. The instrument may then be left in the bladder.

1. **Penis.**—This organ should next bo examined. Tho large dorsal vein will generally bo visible on its upper surface, and on either side of it, in a well injected subject, an artery may be visible. The prepuce should be reflected and its frænum examined. The glans with its corona at its base, and the constricted portion or cervix, around which are collected the glands of Tyson, will then be seen.

2. **Scrotum.**—The spermatic cord should be felt and the vas deferens distinguished from its other constituents, which can easily bo done by its whipcord-like feel. The testicle is of course easily to be felt, and the epididymis lying posteriorly and superiorly should be distinguished from the gland itself. The rugæ of the scrotum are much less distinct in the dead subject than in a healthy living individual, on account of the relaxation of the muscular fibres of the dartos.

A median line or raphe, continuous with a similar line in the perineum, indicates the position where the originally separate halves came together and united in the process of development.

3. **Perineum.**—The scrotum should now be hooked up on the front of the abdomen, and the body placed in the lithotomy position, so that the perineum may be examined. This position is maintained by different methods in different schools, so that no particular

description need be given.   The boundaries of the perineum should first be ascertained.   Commencing in front, the pubic arch, rounded off by the sub-pubic ligament, will be felt, and passing round on either side the rami of the pubis and ischium up to the tuberosity of the latter.   In the middle line behind is the coccyx, and on either side of it the great sacro-sciatic ligament can be distinguished under cover of the edge of the gluteus maximus muscle.   A line from the most prominent part of one tuber ischii to the other divides this diamond-shaped space into two triangles, an anterior or urethral, and a posterior or rectal.   It is divided also by the mesial ridge or raphe, which has already been alluded to.   Like many other middle lines of the body this last is comparatively non-vascular, and incisions should consequently there be made for the escape of extravasated urine.

The central point of the raphe between the scrotum and anus corresponds to the central tendinous point of the perineum or point of junction of the perineal muscles.   This is placed at the centre of the lower border of the triangular ligament, which may be felt on each side of it when the legs are straight and the parts relaxed.   The bulb of the urethra and its artery are always placed in front of this point.   The urethra pierces the triangular ligament about three quarters of an inch in front of it, and its position can be distinctly felt when the sound is within it.

Around the anus, in dissecting room subjects, knots of venous enlargement or piles are not uncommonly the most prominent structures. Apart from these pathological structures, the student will note the radiating folds into which the mucous membrane is thrown, as also a thin white line surrounding the aperture where the skin and mucous membrane join, which indicates the line of division between the external and internal sphincters. By everting the mucous membrane of the rectum slightly, the small pouches, one to three lines in depth, which lie between the ends of the columnæ recti, and are sometimes the seat of ulceration, will be seen.

The left forefinger should now be introduced into the rectum, while the staff is held in the right hand so that it may be moved about when necessary. In the anterior part of the cavity, the student will feel the sound in the membranous part of the urethra. It is here that strictures most commonly occur, and that the catheter requires at times that careful guidance, which, as will now be perceived, the finger in the rectum can give to it. Passing further upwards the apex of the prostate gland will be met with at about an inch and a half from the anus, and the shape of the gland can be explored. About an inch and a quarter higher up the superior border of the prostate will be reached, and the finger having passed beyond it will touch that part of the rectum where the bladder is in contact, without the intervention of peritoneum, and where the operation of tapping per rectum is performed. On each side of this point the common ejaculatory ducts and seminal vesicles may be felt. The lowest of the transverse folds, the valves of Houston or plicæ transversales, may be distinguished on the left side at about the level of the prostate, the next, about four inches from the anus, is on the right side, and roughly marks the lowest point to which the recto-vesical pouch of peritoneum descends. Otis has shown that by placing the dead body in what is known as the knee-elbow position, the rectum becomes dilated by atmospheric pressure, and by suitable illumination (electrical) three or four of these plicæ can be seen placed alternately on either side of the tube. Contrary to a commonly received view he denies that they have any action as valves in holding back the fæces. At the sides of the rectum the finger can explore the ischio-rectal fossæ, and finally behind, near the orifice, the coccyx will be felt. It is sometimes movable in males, generally freely so in women who have borne many children.

Before leaving the perineum the student should mark out the lines of the incisions made in the operations of lithotomy. In the lateral operation the incision is commenced a little to the left of the middle line, and just below the central tendinous point, and is then carried downwards and outwards for two or three inches to a point just below the anus, but one-third nearer to the tuberosity of the ischium than to the margin of that orifice.

In the median operation the edge of the knife is turned upwards instead of downwards, and its point is entered in the middle line about half an inch in front of the anus, and carried onwards until it strikes the groove in the staff which is lying in the urethra.

II. The Female.

The labia majora, covered with hair on the outer surface, and on their inner with mucous membrane, are the first objects visible; they unite below the mons veneris and in front of the perineum, these junctions being known as the anterior and posterior commissures. When these folds are separated, two smaller folds of mucous membrane, the nymphæ or labia minora, will be seen, each being about an inch and a half in length. Traced upwards these will be found to be continuous with the prepuce, covering the glans of the clitoris. Below the nymphæ, and uniting the labia majora, there is in the virgin a transverse fold, the frænulum pudendi, forming with the posterior commissure a triangular area, the fossa navicularis. The student will generally seek in vain for these in dissecting room subjects, as the first parturition usually destroys them. Between the nymphæ is the vestibulum, and in it, about an inch below the clitoris, is the opening of the urethra. A tubercle is often stated in text-books to be placed at this orifice, but as a practical landmark it is almost valueless. Having ascertained the position of the orifice the student should practise passing the catheter. As this operation has to be performed on the living subject without causing exposure, it is well to accustom the fingers to the parts engaged. The subject should be placed on its back, with the knees slightly bent and separated from one another, and the operator

should stand on the left side. The forefinger of the
left hand should be passed down between the vulvæ,
over the clitoris, and into the vestibule, where the orifice
of the urethra may sometimes be felt. In any case,
by passing the point of the catheter along the palmar
surface of the finger, it can, with a little practice, be
made to enter the urethra easily. The ordinary sound
found in dissecting rooms is an inconvenient instrument
for the purpose, but a probe may be used, or still better,
a piece of small sized glass tube about six or eight
inches in length, one end of which has been sealed and
rounded in a flame, and at the same time slightly bent.
When the student has familiarised himself with this
operation, he should leave the instrument *in situ*, and
examine the relation of the urethra, which passes just
below the sub-pubic ligament and the posterior wall of
the bladder to the vagina. The close connection between the walls of these two cavities, and their comparative thinness, leads to their occasional rupture and
the formation of a vesico-vaginal fistula. The same
might be said of the posterior wall, where recto-vesical
fistula occurs. The proper orifice of the vagina is just
below the meatus urinarius, and is generally narrowed
in the virgin by the hymen. This is a structure which
is seldom seen in the dissecting room, but may be
studied in a female fœtus at full term or in the post-
mortem room, in the bodies of virgins. The examination of a sufficient number will teach the student that
it is variable in size and shape. It may even in the
virgin be entirely absent, or represented by a fringe.

On the other hand it may be imperforate, or its opening may be so small as only to admit the point of a probe. The aperture may be enlarged so that the hymen forms a circular ring, but most commonly it is semilunar, with its concavity directed towards the pubis. From all this the student will perceive that any diagnosis of virginity, or the reverse founded upon the condition of the hymen alone, must be very guarded in its nature. After its rupture, small wart-like remains, the carunculæ myrtiformes, may persist, but these generally disappear after a few parturitions.

The forefinger should be passed into the vagina, and the os uteri with the anterior and posterior *cul-de-sac* explored. The posterior is the higher, and corresponds to the pouch of Douglas or recto-vaginal pouch in the cavity of the abdomen. This is the lowest point of that cavity, and the position therefore where fluid will first collect. One forefinger may be passed into the rectum and the other into the vagina, and the wall between examined. At the highest part the recto-uterine fold of peritoneum will lie between the fingers. The description of the anus, mucous folds of the rectum, ischio-rectal fossa, and coccyx, in the male, need not be repeated for the female. Between the anus and the urogenital fissure, lies the perineum of the obstetrical text-books, about one inch in breadth. It is easy to see how the head of the child in parturition may tear through this, and even through the rectum and anus.

CHAPTER VII.

THE BACK.

In the middle line of the back there is a furrow, more or less well-marked, according to the muscularity of the subject, and bounded by muscular masses, which are formed chiefly by the complexus muscle of either side in the cervical region, and by the erectores spinæ in the remainder of the back. At the bottom of this furrow the spines of the vertebræ may be felt, and as Holden remarks, made evident in the living subject to the eye by friction in the median line, when red patches will appear and indicate their position. The spine of the axis may easily be felt beneath the occiput, and that of the seventh or vertebra prominens at the root of the neck, with frequently the spine of the sixth above it. The spines of the vertebræ between the second and the sixth cannot be felt as individual structures, but a ridge indicating their position and that of the ligamentum nuchæ, can distinctly be made out.

The third dorsal spine corresponds to the inner end of the spine of the scapula, and the seventh to the inferior angle of that bone. The twelfth corresponds to the head of the last rib, and the lowest part of the trapezius muscle, which may be made evident in a thin subject by raising the arm and scapula as high as possible. The highest point of the crest of the ilium corresponds to the fourth dorsal spine. On account of the downward direction of the spines of the dorsal vertebræ, these prominences do not all correspond to the rib which belongs to them. The second dorsal spine corresponds to the head of the third rib, and so on, each spine corresponding to the head of the rib of the vertebra below it, until the eleventh and twelfth spines, which are on a level with their own ribs.

The scapula covers the ribs from the second to the seventh inclusive, and its superior and inferior angles and spine can easily be distinguished.

The crest of the ilium and its posterior superior spine can be felt; at the central point of the former there is a triangular space bounded by the latissimus dorsi and external oblique muscles, known as Petit's triangle. The upper limit of the origin of the latissimus dorsi corresponds to a line drawn from the sixth dorsal spine transversely across the scapula.

The trachea bifurcates at a point midway between the third and fourth dorsal spines, the roots of the lungs thus lying a little below and external to that point, the edge of the lung extending as low as the transverse process of the tenth dorsal vertebra. The apex of the lower lobe is at the level of the third rib behind.

Spinal cords and nerves.—The cord extends in the adult from the under surface of the foramen magnum to the lower edge of the first lumbar vertebra as a rule, but it may only reach to the twelfth dorsal, or on the other hand, may be as low as the second lumbar. Its position alters slightly in the movements of the body, as it rises during flexion of the spine. In the child at birth it extends to the third lumbar vertebra. The cervical nerves are named after the vertebra above which they escape, the first nerve emerging above the first vertebra, and the eighth below the seventh, and between it and the first dorsal. The remaining nerves are numbered after the vertebra below which they escape. In relation to the symptoms following upon fractures and dislocations of different parts of the spinal column, it is important to know the point at which each nerve arises from the spinal cord, this point by no means corresponding to that at which it emerges. A diagram showing the relation of the point of exit of the nerves from the cord to that of their emergence from the spinal canal, with the regions supplied by each, will be found in Gower's work on the *Diseases of the Spinal Cord*, and may be consulted with advantage by the advanced student. The following rules relate to the same subject. The first cervical nerve arises from the cord opposite the interval between the atlas and the occiput, the second and third opposite the axis. The fourth to the eighth each arise from the cord opposite the vertebra above the one after which they are named. The first four dorsal nerves arise from the cord opposite the disks below the seventh cervical to the third dorsal vertebræ respectively. The fifth and sixth arise opposite the lower borders of the fourth and fifth vertebræ. The seventh to the twelfth nerves each arise from the cord opposite the vertebra above that after which they are named. The first three lumbar nerves arise from the cord opposite the twelfth dorsal vertebra, and the fourth opposite the disk between the twelfth dorsal and first lumbar vertebræ. The last lumbar, the sacral and coccygeal nerves, arise opposite the first lumbar vertebra. By bearing these rules in mind the student will be able to determine what portions of the body would be affected after an injury to the cord at any given level.

Kidneys.—The kidneys lie on a level with the last dorsal and first two or three lumbar vertebræ, the right being about half an inch or more lower than the left, so that about two inches on the left, and an inch and a half or less on the right, intervene between the lower border of the gland and the iliac crest. The hilus lies from two to two and a half inches from the middle line, and is about opposite the first lumbar spine. In the normal condition it is difficult to feel these organs, but in a thin subject with flaccid walls the rounded outer border may be made out. When abnormally enlarged they may be distinguished, and in searching for them the student should adopt the following method. Stand on the side of the body opposite to the kidney to be examined, pass one hand under the back until the fingers slip over the edge of the erector spinæ muscle of the opposite side, then press backwards with the other hand upon the anterior abdominal parietes, so that the points of the fingers of either hand may be brought as near to one another as possible, when the organ may be felt between them.

Colon.—The ascending and descending parts of the colon can be approached through the posterior parietes of the abdomen in the lumbar region between the crest of the ilium and the last rib, but the operation of colotomy is, for various reasons, generally performed upon the latter. The incision in this operation is made from the edge of the erector spinæ muscle, at a point midway between the crest of the ilium and the last rib, and parallel to the last named structure.

This seems to be the best place to give a table of the relations of certain of the viscera and other structures to the vertebral column, which it is hoped may be useful to the student as a guide to the topography of the parts in and near the middle line.

Cervical.
1. Level of hard palate.
2. Level of free edge of upper teeth.
3 & 2. Superior cervical ganglion of sympathetic.
4. Hyoid bone.
5. Middle cervical ganglion.
6. Cricoid cartilage, end of pharynx, commencement of œsophagus and trachea.
7. Inferior cervical ganglion.

Dorsal.

2. Termination of second part of aortic arch (L). Disk. Level of episternal notch.

3.

4. Level of angulus Ludovici. Lowest limit of superior mediastinum. Termination of arch of aorta (L). Bifurcation of trachea (lower border).

5 to 8. Base of heart.

6. Pulmonary and aortic orifices.

7. Mitral orifice.

8. Tricuspid orifice (R).

9. Level of lower end of manubrium. Openings in diaphragm for vena cava inferior, and œsophagus. 9 to 11. Spleen.

10. Level of tips of xiphoid cartilage. Lower limit of lung posteriorly (transverse process). 10 and 11. Spigelian lobe of liver.

11. Supra-renal capsule.

12. Aortic orifice in diaphragm (upper border) cœliac axis (lower border). 12 to 3 L. Kidney.

Lumbar.

1. Pancreas. Lower end of spinal cord. Superior mesenteric artery (lower border). Hilus of kidney (spine).

2. Upper limit of third stage of duodenum (L). Receptaculum chyli. Renal arteries.

Lumbar.

 8. Lower limit of second stage of duodenum (R).
  Inferior mesenteric artery.

  Disk. Umbilicus.

 4. Bifurcation of aorta. Level of highest point of
  crest of ilium.

  Disk. Ilio-cœcal valve.

 5. Commencement of inferior vena cava.

Sacral.

 3. End of first stage of rectum.

Coccyx, tip.

 End of second stage of rectum.

CHAPTER VIII.

UPPER EXTREMITY.

I. Shoulder and Axilla.

1. Bony points.—The clavicle may be seen and felt in its entire extent. In the ordinary position in men it is not horizontal but slopes upwards from the middle line, the amount of this slope being increased when the weight is taken off the arm as in the recumbent posture. But in women commonly, and sometimes in men also, its slope is downwards from the middle line. The outer extremity of the clavicle leads to the acromion process, which with the spine of the scapula is quite distinct. The tip of the former is one of the prominences from which measurements of the upper limb are made, and it may be remembered that in the hanging position of the arm, the palm being directed forwards, it is in the same line as the external condyle of the humerus and the styloid process of the radius. The student should remember that the end of the acromion process may be unconnected with the spine, by a failure of bony union between the centres from which it and the spine are developed. Under cover of the deltoid muscle the two tuberosities of the humerus will be felt, the greater being external and in the line of the external condyle, the lesser anterior. Between

them the bicipital groove and tendon may sometimes
be distinctly made out.   By placing the hand on the
apex of the shoulder and the thumb in the axilla, and
pressing deeply with the latter, the arm being in the
dependent position, the neck of the scapula and
lower border of the glenoid fossa can be distinguished.
If now the arm be abducted and the thumb moved a
little outwards the head of the humerus will be felt,
and can be easily identified by rotating the arm, when
its shape will be distinctly recognised.   It lies in the
same line as the internal condyle.   By deep pressure
beneath the clavicle in the interval between the deltoid
and pectoralis major muscles, the tip of the coracoid
process will be felt.   This is another point from which
measurements of the upper extremity are made, and is
also valuable as a guide to the axillary artery in its first
stage.

2. **Soft parts.**—The point of the shoulder is capped
over by the deltoid muscle, the limits of which are
easily to be defined.   Under ordinary circumstances it
forms a smooth rounded surface over the subjacent
bony prominences; but in dislocation downwards of the
humerus, and to a lesser degree in paralysis of the
deltoid following upon injury to the circumflex nerve, a
depression will be visible at the outer part of the
shoulder corresponding to the interval between the
head of the humerus and the acromion process.   In the
groove between the deltoid and pectoralis major lie the
cephalic vein and the humeral thoracic artery.   The
coraco-acromial ligament lies under the anterior fibres

of the deltoid, and may there be distinguished, the shoulder joint being immediately underneath it. Under the clavicle is a hollow of variable depth, the sub-clavicular fossa, in which the axillary vessels lie ; it is obliterated or replaced by a prominence in certain dislocations of the humerus. At a lower level the line of division between the clavicular and sternal portions of the pectoralis major may be distinctly seen in some subjects. The student should next examine the axilla and move the arm in different directions so as to observe the alterations in its shape caused thereby. Its base is somewhat triangular, the apex being at the humerus, and the base at the chest wall. The depression between the anterior and posterior folds is deepest when the arm is at an angle of 45° with the chest, and shallowest when the arm is raised above the level of the shoulder. The hollow, however, never quite disappears, a fact which is partly due to the action of the suspensory ligament, a part of the deep fascia connected with the skin below. The skin of the axilla is well supplied with hairs, sebaceous and sweat glands. When the arm is stretched out at a right angle to the body the prominence of the coraco-brachialis muscle may be distinctly seen passing down to the middle of inner border of the humerus. If the arm be maintained in this position and a line drawn from the centre of the clavicle, to the humerus, internal to the lower end of the coraco-brachialis, it will correspond to the axillary artery. This vessel may be compressed in its first stage against the second rib, beneath the clavicle tum. The triceps muscle is the only structure to be studied on the back of the arm ; its details can be seen when a living person forcibly extends the forearm on the arm. The flat tendinous surface below with its pointed upper extremity and the two muscular masses, one arising on either side of it, are then brought into view in a well developed subject.

2. **Elbow.** *a. Bony points.*—The two condyles of the humerus should first be studied. The internal is the more prominent, descends lower, and is further from the line of the articulation than the external (more than one inch as compared with three-quarters of an inch). It can easily be grasped by the fingers as it lies under the skin, and the edge of the trochlear portion of the lower end of the humerus will be felt about three-quarters of an inch from its apex. The internal supra-condyloid ridge can only be traced for a short distance above it, but a sharp fibrous band will be felt under the skin which is the internal intermuscular septum at its lower end. Between the internal condyle and the olecranon is a depression in which lies the ulnar nerve (the "funny-bone" as it is commonly called) and the inferior profunda artery. The external condyle is less prominent, more rounded at its extremity, placed higher and nearer to the joint line. It can be distinctly felt, and especially posteriorly, and the external supra-condyloid ridge can be traced upwards from it for about three inches. It may be mentioned here that in about one out of every fifty arms (Struthers) there is a hook-like process of bone, the supra-condyloid process, above

the internal condyle, which when present can be distinctly felt. The olecranon process is obvious in all positions of the joint, together with the triangular subcutaneous portion of the ulna which passes down from it and is covered by a bursa. The position of this bony eminence with respect to the condyles should be studied in the various positions of the joint. If the thumb and the next two fingers be placed on the three points respectively and the forearm be moved this can easily be effected. It will then be found that in extension the three points lie on the same line, in semi-flexion the olecranon is below the condyles, and in extreme flexion it is in front of them. Thus normally the olecranon is never at a higher level than the condyles. The relation of these points to one another is of importance in the diagnosis of fractures and dislocations at or near the elbow joint. If the point of the thumb be pressed deeply under the muscles arising from the external condyle and forming the outer boundary of the triangular area in front of the elbow joint the head of the radius will be felt, and if the fingers be placed at a corresponding point at the back of the arm it may be grasped and felt rotating beneath them during the movements of pronation and supination. In complete extension a small groove can be distinguished between the head of the radius and the back of the capitellum behind, as the two are not in contact with one another in that position. If the thumb be now shifted a little inwards and deep firm pressure be made, the coronoid process of the ulna will be felt, though not distinctly,

especially in a muscular subject. In extreme pronation the tubercle of the radius may be felt behind a short distance below the head of that bone, though again not distinctly in a muscular subject.

b. Soft parts.—In the semi-flexed condition a curved crease passing from one condyle to the other and concave upwards, the "fold of the elbow," will be first seen. This line does not quite correspond to the articulation but is placed a little above it. The student should next carefully study the position and relations of the large superficial veins, and for this purpose should select a muscular living subject. The vessels may be made prominent, and thus be investigated with greater ease, if a bandage be tied firmly round the arm a few inches above the elbow. It is impossible to adhere closely to regional limitations in this instance, and the veins should therefore be traced up from their origin to the elbow, the student remembering that deviations from the arrangement regarded as normal are very common.

The veins having been made prominent in the manner indicated, the commencement of the first trunk should be sought on the dorsum of the thumb. Above the cleft between the thumb and the index finger this vein is joined by another coming from the back of the latter digit. The combined trunk passes to the flexor aspect of the fore-arm above the wrist, and runs along its radial border, receiving tributaries from both anterior and posterior surfaces. The veins on the ulnar side commence by tributaries which unite above the cleft between the ring and little fingers to form a trunk, the

vena salvatella. This vessel runs up the back of the
fore-arm turning round to its anterior surface below
the elbow, where it is joined by the anterior ulnar vein
which takes its course along the ulnar border on the
anterior aspect. The median vein which runs up the
centre of the anterior surface of the fore-arm is very
variable in size and length. Below the ante-cubital
fossa it receives a deep tributary which cannot be seen
from the surface, and the combined trunk divides into
two, the median basilic which passes inwards to join
the common ulnar and form the basilic vein, and the
median cephalic which taking the opposite direction
unites with the radial to constitute the cephalic vein.
The median basilic lies in front of the brachial artery,
the bicipital fascia intervening between the two vessels,
and is crossed by twigs of the internal cutaneous nerve.
The median cephalic overlies branches of the external
cutaneous nerve. The anatomy of these vessels is not
surgically of such importance as it was in the not very
distant days when phlebotomy was the commonest of
minor operations. As this has, however, still sometimes to be performed the parts concerned should be
considered in this relation. The median basilic is
usually the larger vessel and affords therefore the better
supply of blood but the median cephalic is the safer,
because the former, as has been mentioned is crossed
by nervous fibres which being wounded may cause the
patient to start, and the operator to plunge his scalpel
through the vein into the subjacent artery, the result
being the formation of an arterio-venous aneurism.

The muscular masses in front of the elbow enclose a triangular depression, the ante-cubital fossa. On the outer side is the extensor eminence, the inner border of which is formed by the supinator longus. On the inner side is the flexor eminence with the pronator radii teres externally. At the upper part or base the lower end of the bicipital elevation will be seen, and the tendon of that muscle can be seen and felt easily lying near the centre of the fossa. Passing off from the biceps at its upper end and on its inner side is a fibrous expansion the bicipital fascia which crosses and helps to bind down the flexor muscles. When this is fairly well-marked it can be seen in a thin subject during flexion, as it produces a furrow in the flexor mass about two finger breaths below the internal condyle. The student will notice that when the biceps is brought gradually into action, the globular mass which it then forms commences near the elbow, and ascends towards the level of the pectoralis major. If the finger be pressed into the ante-cubital fossa under the inner edge of the tendon of the biceps, the pulsations of the brachial artery will be felt at a point about a finger's breadth below the line of the internal condyle. The student will feel just below this point the sharp upper edge of the bicipital fascia preventing him from pushing his finger deeply further down towards the apex of the fossa. He should next place his fingers on his own radial artery at the point where the " pulse" is felt and flexing gradually his arm he will feel what an effect is produced upon the blood current by that movement.

If he be fairly muscular he will be able to entirely stop the flow of blood in his radial artery or at least materially to decrease its volume. This fact is of surgical importance in connection with aneurisms of the brachial artery. The radial recurrent artery passes upwards in the groove between the supinator longus to anastomose with the superior profunda. The posterior ulnar recurrent runs on the opposite side between the brachialis anticus and pronator radii teres to anastomose with the inferior profunda and anastomotica. The posterior ulnar recurrent runs upwards to the depression between the internal condyle, and the edge of the trochlea, and the interosseous recurrent takes the same upward course to the interval between the olecranon and the external condyle. The brachial artery itself bifurcates at a point opposite the neck of the radius as a rule, but the student should be on the look out for a high division either of the axillary or brachial trunks, two arteries which may be distinguishable thus existing, a condition which obtains in about one in every five and a half cases. (*R. Quain*).

In the ante-cubital fossa the median nerve lies first internal to the brachial artery. The musculo-spiral nerve, not strictly in the fossa, lies between the supinator longus and brachialis anticus and under cover of the former muscle. As already mentioned the ulnar nerve lies in the depression between the internal condyle and the edge of the trochlea. Over the olecranon lies a bursa which is sometimes enlarged as a result of some special occupation leading to constant pressure upon it, the disease being known as " miner's elbow."

III. FOREARM AND WRIST.

1. Bony points.—The radius can be explored posteriorly throughout its entire length, from its head to its lower end, though less distinctly for some inches below the head than in its lowest part, on account of the muscles which cover it. Externally and anteriorly its styloid process can be distinctly felt a finger's breadth above the upper border of the ball of the thumb. Passing the finger round the back of the lower end, there will be felt, near its centre, a bony prominence, round which turns the tendon of the extensor secundi internodii pollicis, and still further, towards the ulnar side of the forearm, the groove between the radius and the ulna. Anteriorly, only about the lower half of the radius can be made out, and that not very distinctly. The ulna is also very distinct from the olecranon to the lower end posteriorly. The rounded prominence of the latter is very obvious to sight and touch at some little distance above the wrist joint ; internally and posteriorly the styloid process can be felt. The ulna also can only be indistinctly felt on its anterior aspect. The tip of the styloid process of this bone corresponds to the line of the wrist joint, but the styloid process of the radius is placed at a lower level, and corresponds to the scaphoid.

A line drawn from the tip of one styloid process to that of the other would consequently fall below the line of the joint. In order to indicate this it will be necessary to cause the line, joining the two above mentioned points, to form a curve, with its convexity upwards, and half an inch at its farthest point from the straight line alluded to.

2. **Soft parts.** (a) *Muscles.*—A little manipulation along the outer border of the forearm in its lower half will enable the student to feel the tendons of the radial extensors and supinator longus. If the thumb be fully extended, the bellies of the extensores ossis metacarpi and primi internodii pollicis will be seen distinctly as a rounded elevation, crossing the radius in its lower third, downwards, outwards, and forwards; their tendons can be made out close to the lower end of the radius, lying on the bone, and still more distinctly as they pass over the wrist joint. If the fingers of the right hand be laid on the posterior aspect of the left forearm at its lower part, and the left fingers be extended, the tendons of the extensor communis will be felt, and those of the little finger will be distinguished on the ulnar side if that digit alone be brought into action. Still farther towards the ulnar side, the tendon of the extensor carpi ulnaris may be indistinctly made out. Anteriorly, commencing at the ulnar side, the tendon of the flexor carpi ulnaris can be grasped as it lies under the skin, when the wrist is semiflexed and adducted. Extend the hand and the palmaris longus tendon in the centre of the forearm becomes visible in a considerable part of its extent. This muscle is absent once in every ten bodies on the average, and is three times oftener symmetrically absent than asymmetrically (Macalister).

Under this tendon, and on each side of it, the tendons of the flexor sublimis digitorum can be felt by gentle pressure. At their outer border lies the strong, but not very distinctly to be felt, tendon of the flexor carpi radialis, and finally, at the radial border, the tendons of the two first extensors of the thumb, as they cross the wrist joint.

(*b*) *Arteries.*—Just internal to the two last mentioned extensors, the pulsations of the radial artery can be felt against the subjacent radius, this being the position where the "pulse" is generally observed. A line drawn from this point to the outer border of the biceps tendon just below the head of the radius, will indicate the position of the artery. It is fairly superficial through-out, being overlapped above by the inner border of the supinator longus. It is in the line just mentioned that the incisions to tie the artery are made, the edge of the supinator longus and its tendon being the guide to the vessel.

If the wrist be semiflexed to relax the skin, etc., and the fingers be thrust under the tendon of the flexor carpi ulnaris, the pulsations of the ulnar artery will be felt. A line drawn from this point, and curved slightly, so as to be convex inwards, to the same upper point as that given for the radial artery, will indicate the position of the ulnar, which is, however, quite deeply placed in the upper part of the forearm. When it requires to be tied in the upper third of the arm the incision is made along a line drawn from the front of the internal condyle to the outer border of the pisiform, so that the centre of the incision is three fingers' breadth below the internal condyle.

(c) *Nerves.*—The course of the chief nerves of the forearm may be indicated by three lines. That for the median commences just internal to the brachial artery in the antecubital fossa, and is drawn to the centre of the front of the wrist joint, where it lies under or on the ulnar side of the tendon of the palmaris longus. The ulnar nerve is indicated by a line drawn from below and in front of the outer part of the internal condyle, to the outer side of the corresponding artery at the wrist. It meets the artery at the apex of its convexity, that is at the junction of the upper and middle thirds of the arm. The radial nerve is indicated by a line drawn from the outer edge of the upper part of the tendon of the biceps, meeting the artery about two inches below the elbow joint. It accompanies the artery to a point three inches above the wrist joint, where it leaves its vessel, passing to the back of the forearm under the tendon of the supinator longus muscle. The cutaneous nerve supply of the forearm, as well as that of the arm and hand, will be seen from the diagrams (fig. 8), and the student should accustom himself to map out the parts in correspondence with their nerves.

IV. The Hand.

1. **Bony points.**—On the radial side of the hand at the upper part of the muscles of the thumb a bony

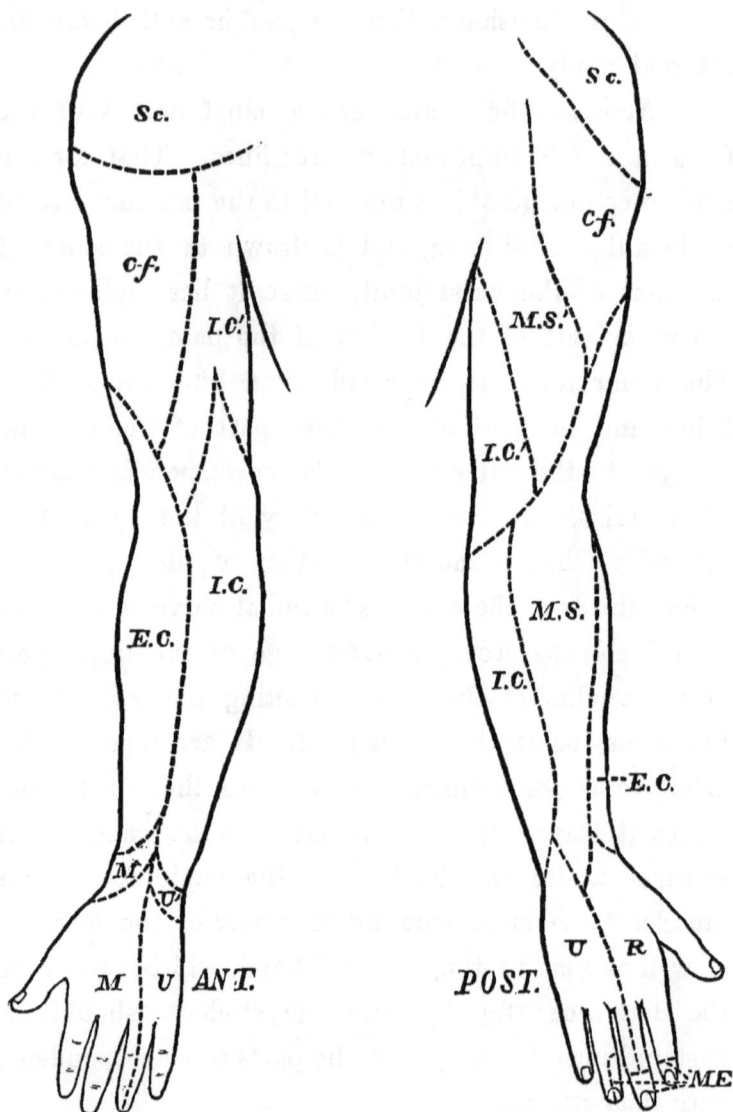

FIG. 8.—CUTANEOUS NERVE AREAS OF UPPER EXTREMITY (Henle).

Sc. Cervical branches.   Cf. Circumflex.   E. C. External circumflex.   I. C. Internal circumflex.   I. C'. Internal and lesser internal
circumflex.   M. Median.   U. Ulnar.   M'. U'. Palmar branches of
median and ulnar.   M. S. Musculo-spiral, external branches.   M. S'.
Internal branches.

NOTE.—According to Suckling's observations the median may
supply the last two joints of index and medius and the radial side of
annularis, as also the last joint of the thumb, all on their dorsal
aspects.

ridge can be made out, which is formed by portions of
two bones, the tubercle of the scaphoid above, and the
ridge on the trapezium below, but any line of division
between the two is hard to distinguish. At the upper
part of the hand, on the ulnar border, the pisiform is
easily identified, and lower down the process of the
unciform may be found, but with less readiness. At
the lower end of the metacarpal bone of the thumb,
and in front of the metacarpo-phalangeal joint, the two
sesamoid bones of that digit can be felt. The lower
ends of the metacarpals of the remaining digits can be
felt in the palm, but not their proximal extremities, on
account of the muscles and other structures lying upon
them. On the back of the hand, since there are less
soft structures between the skin and the bones, the
outlines of the latter can be more distinctly made out.
The upper end of the metacarpal bone of the thumb
can be readily felt, especially if that digit be extended. The upper ends of the metacarpal bones of
the other fingers are not so easy to distinguish, but the
ulnar edge of that of the little finger can be felt at the
border of the hand, if that member be adducted and
pressure be made upwards along the metacarpal until
the point sought for be reached. A line very slightly
curved downwards, drawn from this point to the carpo-
metacarpal joint of the thumb, will correspond to the
line of the carpo-metacarpal articulations. Along this
line the articulations in question may be felt for, that
of the index being distinguishable without much difficulty. The spur on the upper end of the metacarpal

of the middle finger may be indistinctly felt, as well as
the base of the corresponding bone of the ring finger.
Attention should next be directed to the knuckles, and
it will first be noted that in every case the bony
prominence to which that name is attached, belongs to
the proximal bone of the articulation, that is, the first
row of knuckles is formed by the heads of metacarpals,
the second by those of the first phalanges, and so on.
Consequently the line of articulation is somewhat lower
in each case than the corresponding knuckle. The
lines of all the articulations are curved, but the curves
are not all in the same direction. Those of the metacarpo-phalangeal joints are concave towards the wrist,
and are situated from half to three-quarters of an inch
from the free edge of the webs of the fingers. The
lines of the remaining articulations are concave in the
opposite direction, that is, towards the tips of the
fingers, and correspond in their curves fairly accurately
to the curve of the skin surrounding the attached upper
borders of the nails.

2. **Skin and soft parts.**—The hollow of the palm
is somewhat triangular, with its apex directed upwards.
It is bounded by a muscular elevation on either side,
belonging to the thumb and little finger respectively.
The former or thenar eminence is circumscribed by a
groove due to the movement of the thumb in opposition,
which commences on the ulnar side of the fold of skin
uniting the thumb and index finger, and runs upwards
to be lost in the apex of the triangle of the palm. If
the palmaris brevis muscle be made to act, as it can be

in many individuals, an irregular longitudinal crease
will be found along the ulnar border of the hand at the
side of the hypothenar eminence. The apex of the
triangle of the palm corresponds to the lower border of
the anterior annular ligament, the upper margin of
which is indicated fairly accurately by the lower point
of the curved skin crease, which crosses the wrist just
above the two muscular elevations. Another palmar
crease commences close to that of the thumb and passes
across the hand, gradually approaching nearer to the
wrist until it is lost on the hypothenar eminence. Its
radial, most strongly marked portion, is due to the
flexion of the index, the remainder being a secondary
fold caused by flexion of the three inner digits. In the
cleft between the index and middle fingers, another
crease commences, which runs at first upwards and
inwards, as far as the line of the cleft between the next
two digits, and then inwards across the upper part of
the hypothenar eminence. It is the primary fold
caused by the flexion of the three inner digits. The
first of these two last mentioned folds as it crosses the
third metacarpal bone, corresponds to the lowest point
of the superficial palmar arch. Its highest point may
be indicated by a line drawn from the ulnar side of the
commissure of the thumb, when that digit is extended,
transversely across the palm. The digital branches
arise from this arch opposite the clefts of the fingers,
bifurcate half an inch below the webs of the fingers,
and run along the borders of the digits on their palmar
surface, where their pulsations may distinctly be felt

The deep palmar arch lies about half an inch nearer the wrist than the superficial. The second crease crosses the necks of the metacarpal bones, and corresponds also pretty nearly to the upper limits of the synovial sheaths of the flexor tendons of the three inner digits, and to the point where the palmar fascia divides into its terminal slips. The folds at the joints of the fingers should next be examined. Those over the metacarpo-phalangeal articulations of the index and minimus are single, those of the other two digits double. Each is placed about three-quarters of an inch below the joint to which it corresponds. The creases over the first row of interphalangeal articulations are double in each case, and the line of the joint lies between the two. Those of the second inter-phalangeal articulations are single, and lie a very little above the corresponding joints. The thumb is crossed above and external to the thenar eminence by two oblique lines; the lower of these, which commences nearly at the radial side of the commissure, crosses the metacarpo-phalangeal articulation. The line of articulation in the case of each of the joints is more distinct dorsally than on the palmar surface, on account of the flexor tendons, and especially of the so-called glenoid ligaments, which lie between these tendons and the articulations. The flexor tendons of the fingers can be indistinctly felt on the anterior surfaces of the fingers, and the long flexor of the thumb may be distinguished by pressing the finger under the ulnar border of the thenar eminence at its lower end, and extending the thumb. The superficialis volæ artery, when large enough, can be felt pulsating on the thenar eminence. The student will notice that there is no great amount of mobility between the skin in the palm of the hand and the subjacent tissues, a fact which is due to the connection of the former with the palmar fascia. A similar condition obtains at the pulps of the fingers, which is here due to the cutaneo-phalangeal ligaments of Cleland, which pass from the bone to the skin. The result of this immobility of the skin is to give a firmer grasp than would be afforded if the skin glided easily upon the subcutaneous tissues.

On the dorsum of the hand, at the radial side, will be seen, if the thumb be extended, a triangular hollow, "Cloquet's snuff-box," which is bounded radially by the tendons of the two first extensor muscles of the thumb, and on its ulnar side by that of the second internode. In its roof lies the vein which forms the origin of the radial vein of the arm. The base of the metacarpal bone of the thumb lies at its lower part, and the radial artery can be felt pulsating within it. Deeper still lie the scaphoid and trapezium. The princeps pollicis artery can be felt pulsating in the thumb just below the radial end of the commissure, and the princeps indicis in its digit below the ulnar end of the same. Numerous veins are visible on the dorsum of the hand, passing upwards to form the radial or the posterior ulnar trunks. On the radial side of the index the prominence of the first dorsal interosseous muscle or abductor indicis is very distinct. The extensor tendons of the fingers can be seen and felt, and if the fingers be fully flexed, the lateral slips passing from that for the ring finger, to those of the adjacent digits, can also be observed.

CHAPTER IX.

THE LOWER EXTREMITY.

I. The Buttock.

1. Bony points.—The crest of the ilium, which forms the upper boundary of this region, can be felt easily in its entire extent. At its posterior extremity its posterior superior spine will be encountered, lying at the level of the second sacral spine, and corresponding to the centre of the sacro-iliac synchondrosis. The spines of the sacral vertebræ lie in the middle line, and beneath them the tubercles of the last two sacral vertebræ. Just below the last of these, and practically undistinguishable from them, are the cornua of the first bone of the coccyx, the highest point of which process corresponds to the spine of the ischium. The upper border of the great sciatic notch is about on a level with the third sacral spine. The tip of the coccyx can be felt just behind the rectum, and can be grasped between the fingers, if one be inserted into that tube and the other placed on the surface opposite to it. It will be found to be mobile in many women and some men. The great trochanter is easily distinguished, even in fat persons, in whom its position is indicated by a small pit in the soft parts. Its apex corresponds with a point a little above the centre of the hip-joint in

old persons ; in younger individuals, since the neck of
the femur makes a larger angle with the shaft, it is
placed a little lower down.   It is covered by the fascial
insertion of the gluteus maximus, between which and
the bone lies a large and important bursa.

The tuberosity of the ischium can also be readily
felt, especially in the sitting posture, when it comes
from under cover of the gluteus maximus, and forms
with its fellow of the opposite side the main support of
the body.   It is also covered by a bursa, which is one
of three in the body especially liable to inflammation
and enlargement, as a result of occupation.   The
disease commonly known as "Drayman's bottom" is
due to this enlargement.   In connection with certain of
the bony points just mentioned, two methods have been
adopted of determining the position of the trochanter in
relation to injuries at the hips.   The first of these is
known as "Nélaton's line."   This is a line drawn from
the anterior superior spine of the ilium to the most
prominent portion of the tuber ischii of the same side.
It crosses the acetabulum near or above its centre, and
just strikes the apex of the great trochanter.   In dislocations at the hip, the apex of the trochanter will be
either above or below this line.   The second method of
determining the position of the trochanter is known as
"Bryant's ilio-femoral triangle."   This is constructed
by placing the subject in the recumbent position, and
drawing a vertical line from the anterior superior spine
of the ilium.   A second is drawn from the same point
to the apex of the great trochanter, and the third con-

nects the two first. The measurements must be made on both sides, when any increase or decrease of the third or test line on the affected as compared with the normal side can be ascertained.

2. **Soft parts.**—The greater portion of the rounded contour of the buttock is formed by the gluteus maximus muscle. By pushing the fingers upwards beneath the lower border of this, the sharp edge of the great sacro-sciatic ligament can be felt. The lower boundary of the region under description is formed by a distinct crease, the fold of the nates or buttock. This is commonly, but erroneously, said to correspond to the lower margin of the gluteus maximus, but this really crosses the fold obliquely, being higher than it mesially, and lower than it externally. It is not caused by the lower border of the gluteus maximus, as is also often stated, but as was pointed out by Symington, it is largely due to the tuberosity of the ischium, being always best marked where it passes outwards beneath that prominence. The skin is placed on the stretch in flexion of the thigh, and is relaxed during its extension, a fold thus being formed. The position of the arteries of the buttock can be found by means of lines described by Lizar. The first of these is drawn from the posterior superior spine of the ischium to the apex of the great trochanter, the thigh being rotated inwards. The point of junction of the inner and middle thirds of this line indicates the position at which the gluteal artery emerges from the upper part of the great sciatic foramen. The second line is drawn from the posterior

superior spine of the ilium to the outer part of the tuber ischii. Two inches below its upper extremity the line crosses the posterior inferior spine of the ilium, and four inches below the same point, the spine of the ischium. The sciatic artery emerges from the great sciatic foramen, at a point corresponding to the junction of the middle and lower thirds of the line. The pubic artery is, of course, external to the pelvis, as it crosses the spine of the ischium on its way from the greater to the lesser sciatic foramen.

If a line be drawn from the point at which the sciatic foramen emerges, downwards, so as to lie midway between the great trochanter and the tuber ischii, it will correspond to the position of the great sciatic nerve.

The long or inferior pudendal nerve crosses the bone a short distance in front of the tuber ischii, and then curves round into the perineum, to be distributed to the posterior and under surface of the scrotum. The effects of pressure upon this nerve may often be felt in the sensation of " pins and needles " in this region, after long sitting upon a hard surface.

II. The Thigh.

The anterior superior spine of the ilium and the spine of the pubes, both of which prominences have been already alluded to, are the most important bony points in this region. The former is taken as the point from which measurements of the lower extremity are made, and the latter, which is at the same level as the apex of the great trochanter, is an important factor in the diagnosis between inguinal and femoral herniæ. If the two points just mentioned, and the most prominent part of the tuberosity of the ischium, be marked out, the acetabulum will lie about midway between them. Poupart's ligament, stretching in a line curved downwards between the anterior superior spine of the ilium and the spine of the pubes, is easily to be distinguished. The inner inch corresponds to the extent of Gimbernat's ligament.

Crossing the upper part of the thigh, a second line, described by Holden, and usually named after that surgeon, may in many cases be seen, especially if the limb be slightly flexed. It " begins at the angle between the scrotum and the thigh, passes outwards, and is gradually lost between the top of the trochanter and the anterior superior spine of the ilium." When present it runs across the front of the capsule of the hip-joint. The sartorius and adductor longus should be made out as they form the boundaries of Scarpa's triangle. The former is brought into action when the thigh is flexed and adducted, and the latter in abduction, its sharp internal edge, leading to the spine of the pubes, being very easily distinguished.

The femoral artery passes under Poupart's ligament at a point midway between the spine of the pubes and the anterior superior spine of the ilium, where its pulsations may very distinctly be felt. If a line be drawn from this point to the tubercle for the adductor magnus

on the inner condyle of the knee, its upper two-thirds
will overlie the artery. The common femoral divides
into its superficial and deeper portions about an inch
and a half or more below Poupart's ligament. In the
upper third of the thigh the common and superficial
femoral arteries lie in Scarpa's triangle, and are superficial ; below this point they have a deeper position.
Pressure should be applied to the femoral in order to
check its current, backwards and slightly upwards,
below Poupart's ligament, the patient being in the
recumbent position. At the apex of Scarpa's triangle,
pressure should be applied outwards, as the artery is
here on the inner side of the femur.

The femoral vein below Poupart's ligament lies internal to its artery, and has on its other side the
femoral ring and crural canal. The former lies an
inch out from the pubic spine, on a line drawn from
that eminence to the apex of the great trochanter. It
may also be found by ascertaining the position of the
femoral artery by its pulsations, and allowing half an
inch on its inner side for the vein. It is through this
aperture that a femoral hernia escapes from the abdomen, and in the crural canal, along the inner side of
the vein, lie the deep set of femoral glands. The
saphenous opening is placed an inch and a half below
and external to Poupart's ligament, the most important
structure, surgically speaking, which passes through it,
being the long saphenous vein, which will be dealt with
further on. This vessel may sometimes be seen in
thin individuals, the position of the saphenous opening

itself being at times indicated by a dimpling of the skin. Two sets of superficial lymphatic glands lie at the upper part of the thigh, one horizontal and in a line with Poupart's ligament, the other vertical and parallel to the femoral artery. The sources of the various lymph streams which enter these are of some importance, and are thus described in Mr. Treves' *Surgical Anatomy.*

Superficial vessels of lower limb = vertical set.

Superficial vessels of lower half of abdomen = middle glands of horizontal set.

Vessels of inner surface of buttock = internal glands of horizontal set. (A few of these vessels go to the vertical glands).

Superficial vessels from external genitals = horizontal glands, and a few to vertical.

Superficial vessels of perineum = vertical set.

Externally to the femoral artery lies the anterior crural nerve, and under it and the artery, and also external to both, is the ilio-psoas muscle, forming part of the floor of Scarpa's triangle. This muscle overlies the front of the capsule of the hip-joint, a large bursa intervening.

The chief remaining objects worthy of note in the thigh are the muscular markings, of which, besides those which have already been alluded to, the following may be observed. The tensor vaginæ femoris forms an elevation directed downwards and backwards, and commencing at the anterior superior spine of the ilium, immediately behind the sartorius. Below it is inserted

I

into the fascia lata, which in extension of the hip and
knee will be noticed to be particularly tense and re-
sistant on the outer side of the thigh. A specialised
band of this fascia, called the ilio-tibial band, may be
looked upon as the tendon of insertion of the muscle in
question ; it extends down to the outer part of the head
of the tibia, and may be distinctly felt above the knee-
joint, when the muscle is placed upon the stretch.
The rectus femoris forms the median prominence of
the quadriceps and about four inches above the knee-joint
it joins a triangular tendon, which passes downwards
to be attached to the patella. The outline of this
tendon stands out very distinctly in a muscular individual when the knee is fully extended. In the same
position the two vasti muscles are brought into prominence. The lower fibres of the inner descend as low
as the inner border of the patella, those of the outer
not descending so far by an inch or more. A groove
between the inner vastus and the adductor muscles
marks the position of the lower portion of the sartorius
and the subjacent Hunter's canal. A similar groove
on the outer side of the thigh marks the position of the
external intermuscular septum, the line of demarcation
between the vastus externus and the hamstring muscles.

III. The Knee.

The first object which the student should examine is
the patella, and he can, with advantage, in this as in
other parts of the body, carry out his observations upon

himself. In order to examine this bone the leg should be placed in the extended position, the heel resting upon the ground so as to fully relax the muscles and other structures. Its shape can then be fully investigated, and the fingers can even be pushed a little underneath, so as to feel a small part of the posterior surface. It will be noticed that the patella can be moved freely in different directions, gliding easily over the smooth trochlear surface of the femur.

In the same position of the extremity, the whole of the outer border and a part of the upper limit and anterior surface of the articular surface of the external condyle can be felt. In semi-flexion the articular surface of the internal condyle becomes more easy of investigation, when its inner border and a part of its anterior surface can be felt. In extreme flexion the greater part of the anterior surface comes under observation, but not very distinctly, on account of the tension of the skin. Below the patella, and stretching between it and the tubercle of the tibia, is the ligamentum patellæ, which should be studied in the different positions of the joint. If the forefingers of both hands be pushed under the ligament on opposite sides, and alternate pressure be made, a feeling like fluctuation is obtained. This is due to the presence, in that position, of a large pad of fat, lying between the ligament and the subjacent bone, and should not be mistaken for the presence of fluid. In front of the patella and a portion of its ligament, is a large bursa, the prepatellar bursa, which like some others is liable to be enlarged in certain occupations. In the case of the bursa in question, constant kneeling has this effect, and the condition is known as " housemaid's knee." It may be noted that the ligamentum patellæ, the tubercle of the tibia, and the centre of the ankle joint, are all normally in the same straight line. The student should now carefully follow the movements of the patella, and its position in the varying conditions of the joint. He will observe that in extension this bone lies nearly altogether above the articular surface of the femur, its two inferior facets being then in contact with the upper part of the articular portions of the two condyles. In semi-flexion the position of the bones alter so that the patella, resting on its two central facets, lies in contact with a lower part of the condyles. In greater flexion it rests on its two inferior facets. Finally, in extreme flexion, the patella passes almost from off the internal condyle, being turned outwards partly by the increasing prominence of the inner condyle, and partly by the slightly oblique plane, in which the tibia is moved inwards in flexion. It then rests only on its internal narrow facet, which is in contact with the outer border of the inner condyle. Here, as in the other joints of the body, the student should not be content with a dissection of the dead subject, but should take frequent opportunity to examine the bony parts and other structures in all the various positions of the joints in himself and others. He will find much assistance in this study in the descriptions of the mechanism of the articulations in Mr. Morris' work on the Anatomy of the Joints.

The inner condyle of the femur, on its inner side, presents as its most prominent structure the tubercle for the attachment of the adductor longus, the tendon of which muscle can be felt above the projection. The inner aspect of this condyle points nearly in the same direction as the head of the femur. At its lower border the interarticular line between the femur and the tibia can be readily felt. The external lateral ligament can be distinguished on the outer side, passing down to the head of the fibula.

The synovial membrane of the knee joint is more extensive than that of any articulation in the body, and reaches upwards in the extended condition of the limb for two inches or more above the patella. In flexion it sinks considerably, so that in operations about the lower end of the femur there is less danger of opening up the cavity of the knee joint if this position of the limb be adopted.

IV. POPLITEAL SPACE.

The student should first note that the shape of the space varies according to the position of the joint, being flattened out in extension, but hollowed in flexion. Commencing at the outer side, the tendon of the biceps will be felt behind the external lateral ligament. In extension these two structures lie so close to one another that it is somewhat difficult to identify them separately. But if the knee be semi-flexed, the latter will be felt as a distinct rounded cord, whilst the former can be easily grasped beneath the skin. If the fingers be pushed under the inner border of the biceps tendon, a cord-like structure, which is the external popliteal nerve, will be felt. On the inner side of the knee three tendons are to be made out, and may be most easily studied in semi-flexion, with the foot on the ground so as to relax the tissues. The most external and most prominent of these is the semi-tendinosus. Internal to this is what at first appears to be a single tendon, but by a little manipulation the point of the finger can be made to sink into the interval between the semi-membranosus, with its thick rounded border externally, and the gracilis internally.

At the lower part of the space is the angular interval, between the two heads of the gastrocnemius. Between the inner head of this muscle and the tendon of the semi-membranosus is a large bursa, often called the popliteal bursa, though there are several others in that region. In one subject out of every five, according to Holden, this bursa communicates with the cavity of the knee-joint. The popliteal artery in the upper part of the spaces lies to the inner side, under cover of the semi-membranosus. Emerging from under this muscle the artery passes downwards in the centre of the space, terminating opposite the lower part of the tubercle of the tibia. The pulsations of the artery can be felt, and its current checked by compression against the femur in the flexed condition.

The internal popliteal nerve is in the direct continuation of the line of the great sciatic, and lies in the centre of the space.

The lymphatic glands of the space cannot be felt in the normal condition, but when enlarged they are to be made out, and should be remembered, as they may form important factors in coming to a diagnosis in certain surgical conditions.

V. The Leg.

The tubercle and external and internal tuberosities of the tibia are all prominent at its upper extremity, and the large flat anterior subcutaneous surface, which forms the shin, can be traced downwards to the internal malleolus. Its sharp outer border should be felt, and the irregularity of its edge noted. The head of the fibula, with a small part of the shaft below, and the attachments of the external lateral ligament of the knee and the biceps tendon, will be found at the outer side. In the greater part of the leg this bone is hidden beneath masses of muscle, but in the lower third it can be felt again, and becomes subcutaneous over a triangular area above the external malleolus. This triangular area lies between the peronei behind, and the extensors in front.

After the bony points have been fixed the muscular prominences should be studied. The prominence of the calf is mainly formed, so far as is visible from the surface, by the gastrocnemius, the strong tendon of

which can be seen passing down to help to form the
tendo Achillis, behind and above the heel.   If the
muscles of the back be caused to contract, as when the
weight of the body rests on the toes and anterior part
of the feet, the heels being raised from the ground,
the outline of the soleus can be seen on either side of
the upper part of the tendon, but more distinctly on
the outer side of the leg, where it is less overlapped by
the gastrocnemius.   Anteriorly, starting from the outer
border of the tibia, there can be felt and seen, when in
action, first the tibialis anticus, next, and separated
from the former by a groove, the extensor communis
digitorum, a much narrower muscular mass, and finally
the peronei.   In the lower part of the leg the tibialis
anticus and extensor communis digitorum separate
from one another, and here the extensor proprius
hallucis can be felt.

The popliteal artery, as has already been mentioned,
bifurcates at a point opposite to the lower border of the
tubercle of the tibia.   Its posterior tibial branch is
indicated by a line drawn from the point of meeting of
the two heads of the gastrocnemius, to a point midway
between the posterior part of the os calcis and the inner
malleolus.   At its lower part the artery is superficial,
and can be felt pulsating by the side of the tendo
Achillis, but above it is deeply placed.   In the upper
part of the leg, it is reached, for purposes of ligation,
by two methods.   In the first the incision is made
along the inner border of the tibia, and half an inch
behind it, the vessel being thus reached from the side.

In the second, which is called Guthrie's or the military operation, and is comparatively seldom performed, the incision is made in the centre of the calf, the two halves of the gastrocnemius being subsequently separated, and the artery approached directly from behind.

The peroneal branch of the posterior tibial runs along the inner margin of the fibula, on its posterior aspect. The incision to reach it is made along the posterior line of that bone, and rather above its centre.

The anterior tibial artery may be indicated by a line drawn from a point midway between the heads of the tibia and fibula, to a point over the centre of the front of the ankle. The groove, already alluded to, between the tibialis anticus and extensor communis digitorum, is a good guide to this vessel.

The veins of the leg are of great importance on account of the tendency, which for different reasons they possess, of becoming varicosed. The short or external saphenous vein in the normal condition cannot always be seen. It is formed by branches which arise on the outer side of the dorsum of the foot. The trunk when constituted passes behind the external malleolus, runs along the border of the tendo Achillis, lies in the mesial line of the gastrocnemius, and enters the popliteal vein in the popliteal space. The short saphenous nerve lies close to this vein. The internal or long saphenous vein is commonly visible even in the normal condition. It commences by radicles on the dorsum of the foot, passes upwards in front of the internal malleolus, and runs along the inner border of the tibia to

the internal condyle of the knee. Here it lies close to
the bone, and its current is liable to be arrested by
pressure, such as is applied by tight garters or knicker-
bocker bands. From this point it ascends along the
inner and anterior aspect of the thigh, passing through
the saphenous opening into the femoral vein. As far
as the knee it is accompanied by the internal saphenous
nerve, which above this point lies under cover of the
sartorius.

These veins become very visible after prolonged
standing or exercise in the upright posture, and particularly if pressure has been applied to the longer of
the two at the point mentioned above.

VI. The Ankle.

The two malleoli are very important bony landmarks
in relation to this joint, and they present several points
of contrast. The external in the first place descends
half an inch lower than the internal, so that whilst the
line of the ankle joint is about half an inch above the
latter, it is an inch above the former. Secondly, the
external is rather less prominent than the internal.
Thirdly, the external is placed half an inch further
back than the internal, and finally the latter is considerably broader than the former, so that whilst its
anterior border is so far in front of its fibular companion, the posterior borders of the two projections are
on the same line. Owing to the numerous tendons

which pass over the front of the ankle joint, it is rather difficult to feel any of the superior articular surface of the astragalus, but in semi-extension a small portion may be distinguished in front of the external malleolus, and outside the tendon of the peroneus tertius.

The student will notice, in looking at the bones of the foot, that the posterior portion of the superior articular surface of the astragalus is somewhat narrower than the anterior. In the ordinary position of the foot no movements are possible but those of flexion and extension. In the position of extreme extension the narrower part of the superior articular surface of the astragalus lies between the malleoli, and it is stated that at this point a very slight amount of lateral movement is possible. Theoretically, this doubtless is true, but the student by grasping the lower end of the leg with one hand, and the astragalus with the other, the foot being in the position indicated, will be able to satisfy himself that such movement in a muscular living subject is practically non-existent.

A large number of tendons which lie around the ankle joint, and materially contribute to its strength, should next be studied. Posteriorly, the tendo Achillis stands out as the most prominent structure in the region under consideration. Anteriorly, commencing at the tibial side and passing to the fibular, the tendons of the tibialis anticus, extensor proprius hallucis, extensor longus digitorum and peroneus tertius, will be felt in the order mentioned. The best position in which to examine them is that of flexion.

The tendons of the peroneus longus and brevis lie
immediately behind the external malleolus, but are
indistinguishable as separate structures in this position.
Behind the internal malleolus lie, from before backwards,
the tendons of the tibialis posticus, flexor longus digitorum, and flexor longus hallucis.   The first named
can be easily seen and felt, but it is impossible to make
the other two out with any distinctness.

The anterior tibial artery with its nerve lies on the
front of the joint, the latter being external, between
the tendons of the extensores longus digitorum and
proprius hallucis, and its pulsations can here be felt as
it lies upon the lower end of the tibia.

The posterior tibial artery with its nerve, the latter
being external, lies behind the internal malleolus, between the tendons of the flexores longus digitorum and
longus hallucis, and can here be felt pulsating.   The
incision to tie the vessel in this position is made in the
middle line between the posterior border of the tibia
and the tendo Achillis, and parallel to the former.

As the last point in connection with the study of the
ankle and foot, the student should consider the relation
of the parts to the various amputations practised in
that region.   The line of each of these will consequently
be mentioned here, the reader being referred for the
details of each operation to any of the text-books on
operative surgery.

Syme's amputation, which is the one generally performed in the position under consideration, consists in
removing the foot at the ankle joint, and subsequently

sawing off the malleoli with the lower articular surface of the tibia. The two malleoli are the bony guides to the line of the joint in this operation, and consequently their relations to it, as given above, should be carefully borne in mind. In Pirogoff's operation the os calcis is sawn through, the posterior portion being retained in the flap.

VII. The Foot.

1. Bony points.—Along either border of the foot are certain bony prominences, the practical bearing of which will appear when the operations in which they are concerned are described; these points should first be identified.

Commencing posteriorly, there will be felt, along the outer border of the foot, first the external tuberosity of the os calcis, secondly, about an inch below the point of the external malleolus, the peroneal tubercle of the os calcis, thirdly, the spur on the outer side of the base of the fifth metatarsal bone, and finally, the head of the same and the base of the adjacent phalanx.

Along the inner border from behind forwards are:—first, the internal tuberosity of the os calcis; secondly, about an inch below the internal malleolus, the edge of the sustentaculum tali; thirdly, the tubercle of the scaphoid; fourthly, the internal cuneiform bone; fifthly, the base of the fifth metatarsal, and finally the head of the same bone with its sesamoid bones on its inferior surface. Two amputations only need be mentioned through various parts of the foot to show the practical bearing of these points.

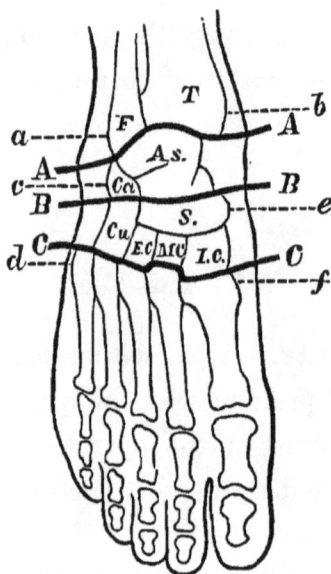

FIG. 9.—DIAGRAM OF FOOT SHOWING BONY PROMINENCES AND LINES OF OPERATION (after Smith and Walsham).

T. Tibia. F. Fibula. As. Astragalus. Ca. Os calcis. Cu. Cuboid. S. Scaphoid. E. C., M. C., I. C. External, middle and internal cuneiform bones. *a. b.* External and internal malleoli. *c.* Peroneal tubercle. *d.* Spur of fifth metatarsal. *e.* Tubercle of scaphoid. *f.* Base of first metatarsal.

AA. Line of Syme's amputation.

BB. Line of Chopart's amputation.

CC. Line of Lisfranc's amputation.

Lisfranc's operation consists in an amputation through the tarso-metatarsal line of articulations. The line of these joints is somewhat irregular, a fact which is chiefly due to the unequal lengths of the three cuneiform bones, but, speaking generally, extends across the foot in a slight curve, with its convexity directed downward, from the base of the fifth metatarsal to that of the first. If, therefore, the student grasps between his fore-finger and thumb the bases of these bones he will have the tarso-metatarsal line immediately behind them. Should he have any difficulty in finding the base of the first metatarsal he may remember that it is placed one and a half inches in front of the scaphoid tubercle, a prominence which is always recognizable.

Chopart's amputation passes through the medio-tarsal joint, between the astragalus and scaphoid, and calcis and cuboid. The guide to the line between the first two bones is the tubercle of the latter. The line of the calcaneo-cuboid articulation lies midway between the external malleolus and the spur on the base of the fifth metatarsal bone.

2. Soft parts.—On the dorsum of the foot the numerous tendons will first claim the attention of the student. Commencing at the inner side the strong tendon of the tibialis anticus will be seen passing downwards, and next to it that of the extensor proprius hallucis, the most prominent of all. Then still further out will be seen the four tendons of the extensor longus digitorum passing obliquely across the foot from within outwards, with the tendon of the peroneus longus lying to the outer side of the tendon for the fifth toe. Externally to this if the toes be extended, a rounded muscular elevation the belly of the extensor brevis digitorum can be seen and felt lying on the front and

outer side of the foot. Its tendons pass under those of
the long extensors in an opposite direction, that is from
without inwards, and may be seen sometimes in thin
persons. On the outer side of the foot the tendons of
the peroneus longus and brevis can be seen and felt.
The former lies behind the peroneal tubercle, the latter
in front of it. The tendons of the inner side cannot be
made out distinctly, though that of the tibialis posticus
with the calcaneo-scaphoid ligament lies in the interval
between the malleolus and the tubercle of the scaphoid.

The dorsal artery of the foot passes over the ankle
joint and runs to the first metatarsal space along the
outer border of the tendon of the extensor proprius
hallucis, where its pulsations may be felt throughout its
entire course. Under the skin over the dorsum a
number of veins will be seen, forming a kind of arch,
the extremities of which form the commencement of the
two saphenous veins.

The metatarsal phalangeal joints lie an inch behind
the skin commissures between the toes.

The skin on the plantar surface of the foot is firmly
adherent to the subjacent structures, so as to permit of
very little mobility. The remarks made as to the use
of this arrangement, and the anatomical explanation of
the same in connection with the skin of the palm of the
hand, will apply also to that now under consideration.

The plantar arteries cannot be seen or felt, but their
position may be marked out by the following rules :—A
point should be taken midway between the tip of the
internal malleolus and the most prominent point of the

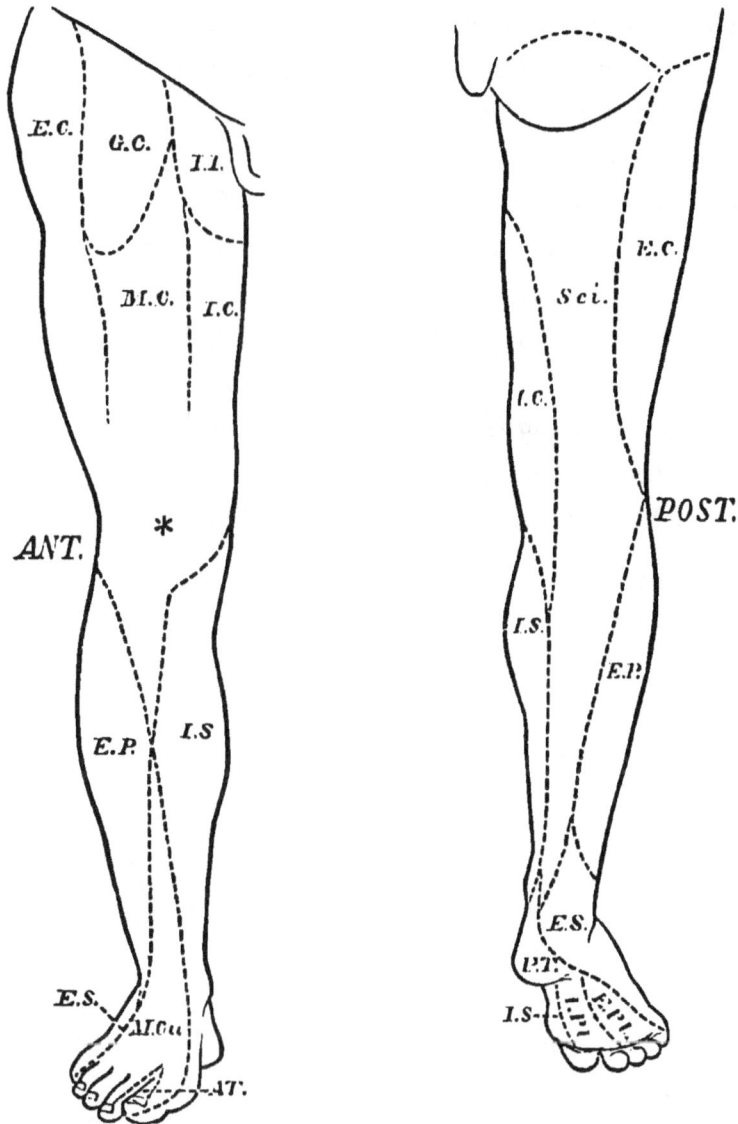

FIG. 10.—CUTANEOUS NERVE AREAS OF LOWER EXTREMITY (Henle slightly modified).

G. C. Crural branch of genito-crural. I. I. Inguinal branch of ilio-inguinal. E. C., M. C., I. C. External, middle, and internal cutaneous. *. Patellar plexus. E. P. External popliteal. I. S., E. S. Internal and external saphenous. M. Cu. Musculo-cutaneous. A. T. Anterior tibial. P. T. Posterior tibial. I. Pl. Internal plantar. E. Pl. External plantar. Sci. Small sciatic.

plantar surface of the heel. A line drawn from this point to the middle of the plantar surface of the toe indicates the position of the internal plantar artery.

A line drawn from the first named point to another one inch internal to the outer border of the base of the fifth metatarsal bone will indicate that portion of the artery which runs longitudinally. From this point it turns and runs across the bases of the metatarsal bones to the first interspace.

Before leaving the lower extremity the student should, as in the case of the upper, map out the areas of the subcutaneous nerves as given in the figures.

INDEX.

A.

Acromion, 85
Angular gyrus, 36
  processes, 2
Angulus Ludovici, 48
Ante-cubital fossa, 94
Apex-beat, 56
Artery, aorta, 58
  abdominal and branches, 69
  axillary and branches, 87-8
  brachial and branches, 89
  carotid, common, 42, 43, 59
    external, 44
  crico-thyroid, 39
  dorsalis pedis, 128
  epigastric, deep, 69
  facial, 6
    transverse, 7
  femoral, 111
  iliac, 69
  innominate, 41, 42, 59
  meningeal, middle, 28
  occipital, 25
  of elbow, 95
  palmar arch, 103
  plantar, 128
  popliteal, 118
  posterior auricular, 25
    palatine, 22
  princeps pollicis, 105
  radial, 98
  subclavian, 42, 45
  superficial temporal, 7
  superficialis volæ, 105
  supra-orbital, 7
  thyroidea ima, 40
  tibial anterior, 121-124
    posterior, 120, 124

Artery, transverse cervical, 46
  ulnar, 98
Ary-epiglottic folds, 21
Asymmetry of face, 10
Asterion, 27
Auricle, left, 55
  right, 56
Axilla, 87

B.

Bicipital fascia, 94
Bladder, 68
Bones of hand, 101
Brachial plexus, 46
Brain, base of, 30
Breast, 51
Bregma, 27
Bryant's ilio-femoral triangle, 108
Buccal pellet, 5

C.

Carotid tubercle, 43
Carpo-metacarpal articulations, 101
Caruncula lachrymalis, 13
Catheter, passage of Eustachian, 16
  female, 75
  male, 70
Chopart's amputation, 126
Clavicle, 85
Clitoris, 75
Cloquet's snuff-box, 105
Coccyx, 107
Colon, 82
Coraco-acromial ligament, 86
  brachialis muscle, 87
Coracoid process, 86
Coronal suture, 28

SELECTED LIST

OF

NEW AND RECENT WORKS

PUBLISHED BY

H. K. LEWIS,

136 GOWER STREET, LONDON, W.C.

. *For full list of works in Medicine and Surgery published by
H. K. Lewis see Complete Catalogue sent post free on application.*

ADOLF STRÜMPELL, M.D.
Director of the Medical Clinic in the University of Erlangen.

A TEXT-BOOK OF MEDICINE FOR STUDENTS
AND PRACTITIONERS. Translated from the latest
German Edition by Dr. H. F. VICKERY and Dr. P. C. KNAPP,
with Editorial Notes by Dr. F. C. SHATTUCK, Visiting Physician
to the Massachusetts General Hospital, etc. Complete in one
volume, with 111 Illustrations, cloth, 28s.   [*Just published.*

"It is to be hoped that this work may prove useful to practitioners and
students alike. It has achieved great success in Germany, having very rapidly
reached a third edition, and has been adopted as the text-book in the Theory
and Practice of Medicine in the Medical Department of Harvard University."
Editor's Preface.

"Prof. Strümpell, lately appointed Director of the Medical Clinic in the
University of Erlangen, is well-known as one of the ablest of modern German
physicians. His system of medicine occupies the same place in Germany at
the present day as did the great work of Niemeyer ten or fifteen years ago."—
Canada Medical and Surgical Journal.

"Of the German text-books of practice that have been translated into
English, Professor Strümpell's will probably take the highest rank. Between
its covers will be found a very complete and systematic description of all the
diseases which are classed under the head of internal medicine . . . . . It is one
of the most valuable works of practice that we have, and one which every
studious practitioner should have upon his shelves."—*New York Medical
Journal.*

DRS. BOURNEVILLE AND BRICON.

MANUAL OF HYPODERMIC MEDICATION. Trans-
lated from the Second Edition, and Edited, with Therapeutic Index of Diseases, by ANDREW S. CURRIE, M.D. Edin.,
etc. Crown 8vo, 6s.   [*Now ready.*

2000—16/3/88

ALFRED COOPER, F.R.C.S.

Surgeon to the St. Mark's Hospital for Fistula and other Diseases of the
Rectum.

A PRACTICAL TREATISE ON DISEASES OF THE
RECTUM. Crown 8vo, 4s.   [*Just published.*

H. CHARLTON BASTIAN, M.A., M.D., F.R.S.

Examiner in Medicine at the Royal College of Physicians; Physician to
University College Hospital, and to the National Hospital
for the Paralysed and Epileptic ; etc.

PARALYSES: CEREBRAL, BULBAR, AND SPI-
NAL. A Manual of Diagnosis for Students and Practitioners. With numerous Illustrations, 8vo, 12s. 6d.

" One great feature of the book is the number of carefully and usefully arranged tables of diagnosis. These are eminently practical, and give the
required knowledge in a nutshell, so that the hard-worked student can get his
food in a concentrated form, and the busy practitioner can keep himself from
rusting, or on emergency refresh his failing memory . . . We can as thoroughly
recommend as we heartily welcome this book."—*Journal of Mental Science.*
" As a special work on the diagnosis or localization of a paralyzing lesion,
we do not know of its equal in any language.'—*Virginia Medical Monthly.*

FREDERICK T. ROBERTS, M.D., B.SC., F.R.C.P.

Examiner in Medicine at the Royal College of Surgeons; Professor of Therapeutics in University College ; Physician to University College Hospital ;
Physician to the Brompton Consumption Hospital, &c.

A HANDBOOK OF THE THEORY AND PRACTICE
OF MEDICINE. Sixth Edition, with Illustrations, in
one volume of over 1000 pages, large 8vo, 21s.

" We heartily commend this handbook, not only to gentlemen prepar-
ing for the medical profession, but to those who have finished their professional
education ; as this work contains, in a brief and concise shape, all that the
busy practitioner needs to know to enable him to carry on his practice with
comfort to himself and with advantage to his patients."—*British Medical
Journal.*
" We have already on more than one occasion expressed a high opinion as
to the merits of this work. . . . . From our experience of the ' Handbook,' we
believe that it will always be popular amongst medical students, and that it is
sufficiently classical to deserve a place on the bookshelves of every physician.
. . . . We heartily commend it as a reliable guide not less to the practical than
to the theoretical study of medicine."—*Dublin Journal of Medical Science.*

BY THE SAME AUTHOR.

THE OFFICINAL MATERIA MEDICA. Second Edit.,
entirely rewritten in accordance with the latest British
Pharmacopœia, fcap. 8vo, 7s. 6d.   [*Just published.*

" In our number for January, 1885, we noticed the first edition of Dr.
Roberts' book, remarking that ' with this compendious book in his hand the
student will have a safe and excellent guide to the official materia medica'.
We say that yet more strongly of the present edition. It is essentially a book
for students who, in the words of the author, will find the subject presented
from every aspect which can fairly be required at examinations."—*Liverpool
Medico-Chirurgical Journal.*

SIR WILLIAM AITKEN, KNT., M.D., F.R.S.

ON THE ANIMAL ALKALOIDS, THE PTOMAINES, LEUCOMAINES, AND EXTRACTIVES IN THEIR PATHOLOGICAL RELATIONS. Crown 8vo, 2s. 6d.

DR. R. ULTZMANN.

ON STERILITY AND IMPOTENCE IN MAN. Translated from the German with notes and additions by ARTHUR COOPER, L.R.C.P., M.R.C.S., Surgeon to the Westminster General Dispensary. With Illustrations, fcap. 8vo, 2s. 6d.

[*Now ready.*

ANGEL MONEY, M.D., M.R.C.P.
Assistant Physician to the Hospital for Children, Great Ormond Street; and to the Victoria Park Chest Hospital.

TREATMENT OF DISEASE IN CHILDREN: Including the Outlines of Diagnosis and the chief Pathological differences between Children and Adults. Crown 8vo, 10s. 6d. [*Ready.*
Lewis's Practical Series.]

" The work presents the charm of originality. The author has expressed his own idea, in his own way. . . . Still as its title implies, the book is chiefly concerned with ' treatment,' and the information given here is full and complete."—*Practitioner.*

" Of Dr. Money's work, which is essentially one on therapeutics, we can also speak highly. It gives a pretty complete exposition of the various methods of treatment which have been recommended by different authorities, and embodies the results of the author's experience at the Great Ormond Street Hospital . . . . His own recommendations are judicious and will meet with general approval."—*Lancet.*

FRANCIS HENRY CHAMPNEYS, M.A., M.B. OXON., F.R.C.P.
Obstetric Physician and Lecturer on Obstetric Medicine at St. George's Hospital ; Examiner in Obstetric Medicine in the University of London, etc.

EXPERIMENTAL RESEARCHES IN ARTIFICIAL RESPIRATION IN STILLBORN CHILDREN, AND ALLIED SUBJECTS. Crown 8vo, 3s. 6d.

HENRY DAVIS, M.R.C.S. ENG.
Teacher and Administrator of Anæsthetics to St. Mary's and the National Dental Hospitals.

GUIDE TO THE ADMINISTRATION OF ANÆSTHETICS. Fcap. 8vo, 2s.

BERKELEY HILL, M.B. LOND., F.R.C.S.
Professor of Clinical Surgery in University College; Surgeon to University College Hospital, and to the Lock Hospital.

AND

ARTHUR COOPER, L.R.C.P., M.R.C.S.
Surgeon to the Westminster General Dispensary, &c.

I.

SYPHILIS AND LOCAL CONTAGIOUS DISORDERS. Second Edition, entirely re-written, royal 8vo, 18s.

II.

THE STUDENT'S MANUAL OF VENEREAL DISEASES. Being a Concise Description of those Affections and of their Treatment. Fourth Edition, post 8vo, 2s. 6d.

SYDNEY RINGER, M.D., F.R.S.
Professor of the Principles and Practice of Medicine in University College; Physician to, and Professor of Clinical Medicine in, University College Hospital.

A HANDBOOK OF THERAPEUTICS. Eleventh Edition, revised, 8vo, 15s.

" .... The work supplies a felt want, giving useful information which can be obtained from no other book, and which is of the utmost value in practice... The work has now become almost indispensable both to students of medicine and to practitioners."—*Practitioner*
" It is unquestionably the ablest work on Therapeutics which we possess in our language, and one which should be carefully perused not only by students, but also by practitioners....Ringer's *Therapeutics* is so well-known that it needs no commendation from us to ensure it a wide circulation."—*Edinburgh Medical Journal.*

R. DOUGLAS POWELL, M.D., F.R.C.P., M.R.C.S.
Physician to the Hospital for Consumption and Diseases of the Chest at Brompton, Physician to the Middlesex Hospital.

DISEASES OF THE LUNGS AND PLEURÆ INCLUDING CONSUMPTION. Third Edition, re-written and enlarged, with coloured plates and wood-engravings, 8vo, 16s.

" We commend this book as one which should be in the hands of every practitioner. It is plainly the outcome of wide experience, and it has been written in a thoughtful and practical manner, so that no one who studies its pages can fail to derive therefrom much that will stand him in good stead at the bedside."—*Lancet.*
" The present edition will take a high place in the estimation of practical physicians. Over and beyond the wide knowledge displayed and the judicial temper with which disputed points are discussed, there remains a striking characteristic of the book, which may perhaps be best called its helpfulness; difficulties in practice are honestly stated and sound practical advice is given, to the exculsion of vague generalisation or hearsay recommendations of new nostrums."—*British Medical Journal.*

ROBSON ROOSE, M.D., F.R.C.P. EDIN.

GOUT, AND ITS RELATIONS TO DISEASES OF THE LIVER AND KIDNEYS. Fifth Edition, crown 8vo, 3s. 6d. [*Just published.*

C. W. MANSELL MOULLIN, M.A., M.D. OXON., F.R.C.S. ENG.
Assistant Surgeon and Senior Demonstrator of Anatomy at the London Hospital; formerly Radcliffe Travelling Fellow and Fellow of Pembroke College, Oxford.

SPRAINS; THEIR CONSEQUENCES AND TREATMENT. Crown 8vo, 5s. [*Now ready.*

LEWIS A. STIMSON, B.A., M.D.
Surgeon to the Presbyterian and Bellevue Hospitals; Professor of Clinical Surgery in the Medical Faculty of the University of the City of New York, etc.

A MANUAL OF OPERATIVE SURGERY. With three hundred and forty-two Illustrations. Second Edition, post 8vo, 10s. 6d.

HENRY R. SWANZY, A.M., M.B., F.R.C.S.I.
Examiner in Ophthalmic Surgery at the Royal College of Surgeons, Ireland; Surgeon to the National Eye and Ear Infirmary, Dublin; Ophthalmic Surgeon to the Adelaide Hospital, Dublin; Formerly Assistant to the late Professor A. von Graefe, Berlin.

A HANDBOOK OF DISEASES OF THE EYE AND THEIR TREATMENT. Second Edition, Illustrated with Wood Engravings, Colour Tests, etc., large post 8vo. [*In preparation.*

" This is an excellent textbook, written by a surgeon of large experience and a thorough knowledge of the literature of his subject."— *The Edinburgh Medical Journal.*

EDGAR M. CROOKSHANK, M.B. LOND., F.R.M.S.
Professor of Bacteriology, King's College, London.

I.

MANUAL OF BACTERIOLOGY: BEING AN INTRODUCTION TO PRACTICAL BACTERIOLOGY. Illustrated with coloured plates from original drawings and numerous coloured illustrations embodied in the text. Second Edition, 8vo, 21s. [*Now ready.*

II.

PHOTOGRAPHY OF BACTERIA Illustrated with 86 Photographs reproduced in autotype and numerous wood engravings, royal 8vo, 12s. 6d. [*Now ready.*

BERKELEY HILL, M.B. LOND., F.R.C.S.
Professor of Clinical Surgery in University College; Surgeon to University College Hospital, and to the Lock Hospital.

THE ESSENTIALS OF BANDAGING. For Managing Fractures and Dislocations; for administering Ether and Chloroform; and for using other Surgical Apparatus. Sixth Edition, with Illustrations, fcap. 8vo, 5s.

CHARLES CREIGHTON, M.D.

I.

ILLUSTRATIONS OF UNCONSCIOUS MEMORY IN DISEASE, including a Theory of Alteratives. Post 8vo, 6s.

II.

CONTRIBUTIONS TO THE PHYSIOLOGY AND PATHOLOGY OF THE BREAST AND LYMPHATIC GLANDS. Second Edition, with wood-cuts and plate, 8vo, 9s.

III.

BOVINE TUBERCULOSIS IN MAN: An Account of the Pathology of Suspected Cases. With Chromo-lithographs and other Illustrations, 8vo, 8s. 6d.

W. H. O. SANKEY, M.D. LOND., F.R.C.P.
Late Lecturer on Mental Diseases, University College, and School of Medicine for Women, London.

LECTURES ON MENTAL DISEASE. Second Edition, with coloured plates, 8vo, 12s. 6d.

ROBERTS BARTHOLOW, M.A., M.D., LL.D.
Professor of Materia Medica and Therapeutics in the Jefferson Medical College of Philadelphia, etc.

I.

A TREATISE ON THE PRACTICE OF MEDICINE FOR THE USE OF STUDENTS AND PRACTITIONERS. With Illustrations, 5th Edition, large 8vo, 21s.

II.

A PRACTICAL TREATISE ON MATERIA MEDICA AND THERAPEUTICS. Sixth Edition, Revised and Enlarged, 8vo, 18s.   [*Just published.*

8   New and Recent Works published by

FANCOURT BARNES, M.D., M.R.C.P.
Physician to the Chelsea Hospital; Obstetric Physician to the Great
Northern Hospital, &c.

A GERMAN-ENGLISH DICTIONARY OF WORDS
AND TERMS USED IN MEDICINE AND ITS
COGNATE SCIENCES. Square 12mo, Roxburgh binding, 9s.

ALFRED H. CARTER, M.D. LOND.
Member of the Royal College of Physicians; Physician to the Queen's
Hospital, Birmingham; Examiner in Medicine for the
University of Aberdeen, &c.

ELEMENTS OF PRACTICAL MEDICINE. Fourth
Edition, crown 8vo, 9s.

P. CAZEAUX.
Adjunct Professor in the Faculty of Medicine of Paris, &c.

AND

S. TARNIER.
Professor of Obstetrics and Diseases of Women and Children in the Faculty
of Medicine of Paris.

OBSTETRICS: THE THEORY AND PRACTICE;
including the Diseases of Pregnancy and Parturition, Obstetrical Operations, &c. Seventh Edition, edited and revised by
ROBERT J. HESS, M.D., with twelve full-page plates, five being
coloured, and 165 wood-engravings, 1081 pages, royal 8vo, 35s.

W. H. CORFIELD, M.A., M.D. OXON.
Professor of Hygiene and Public Health in University College, London.

DWELLING HOUSES: their Sanitary Construction and
Arrangements. Second Edition, with Illustrations, crown
8vo, 3s. 6d.

EDWARD COTTERELL, M.R.C.S. ENG., L.R.C.P. LOND.
Late House Surgeon, University College Hospital; Atkinson Morley Surgical
Scholar, University College, London, etc.

ON SOME COMMON INJURIES TO LIMBS: their
Treatment and After-Treatment including Bone-Setting (so-
called). Imp. 16mo, with Illustrations, 3s. 6d.

WM. JAPP SINCLAIR, M.A., M.D.

Hon. Physician to the Manchester Southern Hospital for Women and
Children and Manchester Maternity Hospital.

O^N GONORRHŒAL INFECTION IN WOMEN.
Post 8vo.   [*In the press.*

J. MAGEE FINNEY, M.D. DUBLIN.

King's Professor of Practice of Medicine in School of Physic, Ireland;
Clinical Physician to Sir Patrick Dun's Hospital.

N^{OTES} ON THE PHYSICAL DIAGNOSIS OF LUNG
DISEASES. 32mo, 1s. 6d.

J. MILNER FOTHERGILL, M.D.

Member of the Royal College of Physicians of London; Physician to the City
of London Hospital for Diseases of the Chest, Victoria Park, &c.

I.

A MANUAL OF DIETETICS. Large 8vo, 10s. 6d.

II.

T^{HE} HEART AND ITS DISEASES, WITH THEIR
TREATMENT; INCLUDING THE GOUTY HEART.
Second Edition, entirely re-written, copiously illustrated with
woodcuts and lithographic plates.   8vo, 16s.

III.

I^{NDIGESTION}, BILIOUSNESS, AND GOUT IN ITS
PROTEAN ASPECTS.

PART I.—INDIGESTION AND BILIOUSNESS. Second
Edition, post 8vo, 7s. 6d.   [*Just published.*
PART II.—GOUT IN ITS PROTEAN ASPECTS.
Post 8vo, 7s. 6d.

ALFRED W. GERRARD, F.C.S.

Pharmaceutical Chemist; Examiner to the Pharmaceutical Society; Teacher
of Pharmacy and Demonstrator of Materia Medica to University
College Hospital, etc.

E^{LEMENTS} OF MATERIA MEDICA AND PHAR-
MACY.   Crown 8vo, 8s. 6d.

L^{EWIS'S} POCKET CASE BOOK FOR PRACTI-
TIONERS AND STUDENTS. Designed by A. T.
BRAND, M.D. Roan, with pencil, 3s. 6d. *nett.*

LEWIS'S PRACTICAL SERIES.

Under this title Mr. Lewis is publishing a complete series of Monographs embracing the various branches of Medicine and Surgery.

·The volumes, written by well-known Hospital Physicians and Surgeons recognised as authorities in the subjects of which they treat, are in active preparation. ·The works are intended to be of a thoroughly Practical nature, calculated to meet the requirements of the general Practitioner, and to present the most recent information in a compact and readable form; the volumes will be handsomely got up and issued at low prices, varying with the size of the works.

THE FOLLOWING ARE NOW READY.

TREATMENT OF DISEASE IN CHILDREN: INCLUDING THE OUTLINES OF DIAGNOSIS AND THE CHIEF PATHOLOGICAL DIFFERENCES BETWEEN CHILDREN AND ADULTS. By ANGEL MONEY, M.D., M.R.C.P., Assistant Physician to the Hospital for Children, Great Ormond Street, and to University College Hospital. Crown 8vo, 10s. 6d.   [*Ready.*

ON FEVERS: THEIR HISTORY, ETIOLOGY, DIAGNOSIS, PROGNOSIS, AND TREATMENT. By ALEXANDER COLLIE, M.D. (Aberdeen), Member of the Royal College of Physicians of London; Medical Superintendent of the Eastern Hospitals; Secretary of the Epidemiological Society for Germany and Russia. Coloured plates, cr. 8vo, 8s. 6d.

HANDBOOK OF DISEASES OF THE EAR FOR THE USE OF STUDENTS AND PRACTITIONERS. By URBAN PRITCHARD, M.D. (Edin.), F.R.C.S. (Eng.), Professor of Aural Surgery at King's College, London; Aural Surgeon to King's College Hospital; Senior Surgeon to the Royal Ear Hospital. With Illustrations, crown 8vo, 4s. 6d.

A PRACTICAL TREATISE ON DISEASES OF THE KID-NEYS AND URINARY DERANGEMENTS. By C. H. RALFE, M.A., M.D. Cantab., F.R.C.P. Lond., Assistant Physician to the London Hospital, late Senior Physician to the Seamen's Hospital, Greenwich. With Illustrations, crown 8vo, 10s. 6d.

DENTAL SURGERY FOR GENERAL PRACTITIONERS AND STUDENTS OF MEDICINE. By ASHLEY W. BARRETT, M.B. Lond., M.R.C.S., L.D.S., Dental Surgeon to, and Lecturer on Dental Surgery and Pathology in the Medical School of, the London Hospital. With Illustrations, crown 8vo, 3s.

BODILY DEFORMITIES AND THEIR TREATMENT: A Handbook of Practical Orthopædics. By H. A. REEVES, F.R.C.S. Ed., Senior Assistant Surgeon and Teacher of Practical Surgery at the London Hospital; Surgeon to the Royal Orthopædic Hospital, etc. With numerous Illustrations, crown 8vo, 8s. 6d.

₊ Prospectus of the Series, with Specimen pages, etc., post free on application.

L EWIS'S POCKET MEDICAL VOCABULARY. Over 200 pp., 32mo, limp roan, 3s. 6d.

HENEAGE GIBBES, M.D.

Lecturer on Physiology and on Normal and Morbid Histology in the Medical School of Westminster Hospital; etc.

PRACTICAL HISTOLOGY AND PATHOLOGY.
Third Edition, revised and enlarged, crown 8vo, 6s.

J. B. GRESSWELL, M.R.C.V.S.

Provincial Veterinary Surgeon to the Royal Agricultural Society.

VETERINARY PHARMACOLOGY AND THERAPEUTICS. Fcap. 8vo, 5s.

J. WICKHAM LEGG, F.R.C.P.

Assistant Physician to Saint Bartholomew's Hospital, and Lecturer on Pathological Anatomy in the Medical School.

I.

ON THE BILE, JAUNDICE, AND BILIOUS DISEASES. With Illustrations in chromo-lithography, 719 pages, roy. 8vo, 25s.

II.

A GUIDE TO THE EXAMINATION OF THE URINE; intended chiefly for Clinical Clerks and Students. Sixth Edition, revised and enlarged, with additional Illustrations, fcap. 8vo, 2s 6d.

WILLIAM THOMPSON LUSK, A.M., M.D.

Professor of Obstetrics and Diseases of Women in the Bellevue Hospital Medical College, &c.

THE SCIENCE AND ART OF MIDWIFERY. Third Edition, revised and enlarged, with numerous Illustrations, 8vo, 18s.

PATRICK MANSON, M.D., C.M.
Amoy, China.

THE FILARIA SANGUINIS HOMINIS AND CERTAIN NEW FORMS OF PARASITIC DISEASE IN INDIA, CHINA, AND WARM COUNTRIES. Illustrated with Plates, Woodcuts, and Charts. Demy 8vo, 10s. 6d.

WILLIAM MARTINDALE, F.C.S.
Late Examiner of the Pharmaceutical Society, and late Teacher of Pharmacy and Demonstrator of Materia Medica at University College.

AND

W. WYNN WESTCOTT, M.B. LOND.
Deputy Coroner for Central Middlesex.

THE EXTRA PHARMACOPŒIA with the additions introduced into the British Pharmacopœia 1885; and Medical References, and a Therapeutic Index of Diseases and Symptoms. Fourth Edition, revised, limp roan, med. 24mo, 7s.
[*Now ready.*

A. STANFORD MORTON, M.B., F.R.C.S. ED.
Senior Assistant Surgeon, Royal South London Ophthalmic Hospital.

REFRACTION OF THE EYE: Its Diagnosis, and the Correction of its Errors, with Chapter on Keratoscopy. Third Edition. Small 8vo, 3s.

WILLIAM MURRELL, M.D., F.R.C.P.
Lecturer on Materia Medica and Therapeutics at Westminster Hospital Examiner in Materia Medica and Therapeutics in the University of Edinburgh, and to the Royal College of Physicians, London.

I.

MASSAGE AS A MODE OF TREATMENT. Third Edition, crown 8vo, 4s. 6d.   [*Just published.*

II.

WHAT TO DO IN CASES OF POISONING. Fifth Edition, royal 32mo, 3s. 6d.

G. OLIVER, M.D., M.R.C.P.

I.

ON BEDSIDE URINE TESTING: a Clinical Guide to the Observation of Urine in the course of Work. Third Edition, considerably enlarged, fcap. 8vo, 3s. 6d.

II.

THE HARROGATE WATERS: Data Chemical and Therapeutical, with notes on the Climate of Harrogate. Addressed to the Medical Profession. Crown 8vo, with Map of the Wells, 3s. 6d.

R. W. PARKER.
Surgeon to the East London Hospital for Women and Children and to the Grosvenor Hospital for Women and Children.

I.

TRACHEOTOMY IN LARYNGEAL DIPHTHERIA; AFTER - TREATMENT AND COMPLICATIONS. Second Edition, with Illustrations, 8vo, 5s.

II.

CONGENITAL CLUB-FOOT: ITS NATURE AND TREATMENT. With special reference to the subcutaneous division of Tarsal Ligaments. 8vo, 7s. 6d.

G. V. POORE, M.D., F.R.C.P.
Professor of Medical Jurisprudence, University College; Assistant Physician and Physician in charge of the Throat Department of University College Hospital.

LECTURES ON THE PHYSICAL EXAMINATION OF THE MOUTH AND THROAT. With an appendix of Cases. 8vo, 3s. 6d.

CHARLES W. PURDY, M.D. (QUEEN'S UNIV.)
Professor of Genito-Urinary and Renal Diseases in the Chicago Polyclinic, etc., etc.

BRIGHT'S DISEASE AND THE ALLIED AFFECTIONS OF THE KIDNEYS. With Illustrations, large 8vo, 8s. 6d.

D. B. ST. JOHN ROOSA, M.A., M.D.
Professor of Diseases of the Eye and Ear in the University of the City of New York; Surgeon to the Manhattan Eye and Ear Hospital; Consulting Surgeon to the Brooklyn Eye and Ear Hospital, &c., &c.

A PRACTICAL TREATISE ON THE DISEASES OF THE EAR, including the Anatomy of the Organ. Sixth Edition, Illustrated by wood engravings and chromo-lithographs, large 8vo, 25s.

W. JULIUS MICKLE, M.D., M.R.C.P. LOND.
Medical Superintendent, Grove Hall Asylum, London, etc.

GENERAL PARALYSIS OF THE INSANE, Second Edition, enlarged and rewritten, 8vo, 14s.

JOHN SAVORY.
Member of the Society of Apothecaries, London.

A COMPENDIUM OF DOMESTIC MEDICINE AND COMPANION TO THE MEDICINE CHEST. Intended as a source of easy reference for Clergymen, Master Mariners, and Travellers; and for Families resident at a distance from professional assistance. Tenth Edition, fcap. 8vo, 5s.

[Now ready.

ALDER SMITH, M.B. LOND., F.R.C.S.
Resident Medical Officer, Christ's Hospital, London.

RINGWORM: ITS DIAGNOSIS AND TREATMENT. Third Edition, rewritten and enlarged, with Illustrations, fcap. 8vo, 5s. 6d.

FRANCIS W. SMITH, M.B., B.S.

THE SALINE WATERS OF LEAMINGTON: Chemically, Therapeutically, and Clinically Considered; with Observations on the Climate of Leamington. Second Edition, with Illustrations, crown 8vo, 1s. *nett.*

C. W. SUCKLING, M.D. LOND., M.R.C.P.
Professor of Materia Medica and Therapeutics at the Queen's College, Physician to the Queen's Hospital, Birmingham, etc.

ON THE DIAGNOSIS OF DISEASES OF THE BRAIN, SPINAL CORD, AND NERVES. With Illustrations, crown 8vo, 8s. 6d. *[Just published.*

JOHN BLAND SUTTON, F.R.C.S.
Lecturer on Comparative Anatomy, Senior Demonstrator of Anatomy, and Assistant Surgeon to the Middlesex Hospital; Erasmus Wilson Lecturer, Royal College of Surgeons, England.

LIGAMENTS: THEIR NATURE AND MORPHOLOGY. Wood engravings, post 8vo, 4s. 6d.

FREDERICK TREVES, F.R.C.S.
Hunterian Professor at the Royal College of Surgeons of England; Surgeon to, and Lecturer on Anatomy at, the London Hospital.

THE ANATOMY OF THE INTESTINAL CANAL AND PERITONEUM IN MAN. Hunterian Lectures, 1885. 4to, 2s. 6d.

JOHN R. WARDELL, M.D., F.R.C.P.
Late Consulting Physician to Tunbridge Wells General Hospital.

CONTRIBUTIONS TO PATHOLOGY AND THE PRACTICE OF MEDICINE. Medium 8vo, 21s.

FRANCIS WELCH, F.R.C.S.
Surgeon-Major, A.M.D.

ENTERIC FEVER: its Prevalence and Modifications; Etiology; Pathology and Treatment; as illustrated by Army Data at Home and Abroad. Demy 8vo, 5s. 6d.

DAVID YOUNG, M.C., M.B., M.D.
Licentiate of the Royal College of Physicians, Edinburgh; Licentiate of the Royal College of Surgeons, Edinburgh; Fellow of, and late Examiner in Midwifery to, the University of Bombay, etc.

ROME IN WINTER AND THE TUSCAN HILLS IN SUMMER. A Contribution to the Climate of Italy. Small 8vo, 6s.

HERMANN VON ZEISSL, M.D.
Late Professor at the Imperial Royal University of Vienna.

OUTLINES OF THE PATHOLOGY AND TREATMENT OF SYPHILIS AND ALLIED VENEREAL DISEASES. Second Edition, Revised by M. VON ZEISSL, M.D., Privat-Docent for Diseases of the Skin and Syphilis at the Imperial Royal University of Vienna. Translated, with Notes, by H. RAPHAEL, M.D., Attending Physician for Diseases of Genito-Urinary Organs and Syphilis, Bellevue Hospital, Out-Patient Department. Large 8vo, 18s. [*Just published.*]

CLINICAL CHARTS FOR TEMPERATURE OBSERVATIONS, ETC. Arranged by W. RIGDEN, M.R.C.S. Price 7s. per 100, 1s. per doz., 15s. per 250, 28s. per 500, 50s. per 1000.

Each Chart is arranged for four weeks, and is ruled at the back for making notes of cases; they are convenient in size, and are suitable both for hospital and private practice.

PERIODICAL WORKS PUBLISHED BY H. K. LEWIS.

THE NEW SYDENHAM SOCIETY'S PUBLI-CATIONS. Annual Subscription, One Guinea. Report of the Society, with Complete List of Works and other information, gratis on application.

THE NEW YORK MEDICAL JOURNAL. A Weekly Review of Medicine. Annual Subscription, One Guinea, post free.

THE THERAPEUTIC GAZETTE. A Monthly Journal, devoted to the Science of Pharmacology, and to the introduction of New Therapeutic Agents. Edited by Drs. H. C. Wood and R. M. Smith. Annual Subscription, 10s., post free.

THE GLASGOW MEDICAL JOURNAL. Published Monthly. Annual Subscription, 20s., post free. Single numbers, 2s. each.

LIVERPOOL MEDICO-CHIRURGICAL JOURNAL, including the Proceedings of the Liverpool Medical Institution. Published twice yearly, 3s. 6d. each number.

THE INDIAN MEDICAL JOURNAL. A Journal of Medical and Sanitary Science specially devoted to the Interests of the Medical Services. Annual Subscription, 24s., post free.

MIDDLESEX HOSPITAL. Reports of the Medical, Surgical, and Pathological Registrars for 1883 to 1886. Demy 8vo, 2s. 6d. *nett* each volume.

TRANSACTIONS OF THE COLLEGE OF PHYSICIANS OF PHILA-DELPHIA. Volumes I. to VI., 8vo, 10s. 6d. each.

*** MR. LEWIS is in constant communication with the leading publishing firms in America and has transactions with them for the sale of his publications in that country. Advantageous arrangements are made in the interests of Authors for the publishing of their works in the United States.

MR. LEWIS's publications can be procured of any Bookseller in any part of the world.

Complete Catalogue of Publications post free on application.

Printed by H. K. Lewis, Gower Street, London, W.C.

www.ingramcontent.com/pod-product-compliance
Lightning Source LLC
Chambersburg PA
CBHW020549270326
41927CB00006B/779